MW00640636

OTHERFUL

OTHERFUL

How To Change The World
(and Your School) Through Other People

Mike Kleba & Ryan O'Hara

Candido Press

To Molly and Colleen

No one is alone.

—Stephen Sondheim

"We must have the courage
to ask for help and
to request feedback to
expand our vision
of what's possible.
—MARIA CASTAÑÓN MOATS

Your district is lucky to have you.
Mike Koh.

otherful *(adjective)*

1. A leader who spots the greatness of others

2. A leadership style that recognizes that
    - People don't want to be fixed; they want to be helped
    - Leaders need their people more than their people need them
    - How others understand things isn't an obstacle but, instead, a resource

CONTENTS

WHO WE ARE AND
WHY WE WROTE THIS

Late May, 2010. Lights up on a small office with no windows in a high school not far from New York City. No air conditioning. The fluorescent lights are shut off and an old lamp warms pictures of theatre productions on the walls. Overstuffed bookshelves lean over two massive metal desks one might imagine finding in a building in a neglected Soviet republic. A shabby prop couch left from an old school play. Frank Sinatra sings quietly from a scratched vinyl on an old record player in the corner.

Two public school teachers are talking in the soft light.

O'HARA: Well, that faculty meeting sucked.

KLEBA: I can't do these anymore.

O'HARA: You think HE thinks it went well?

KLEBA: I'm not even sure he wanted to have that meeting himself.

O'HARA: There has to be a better way to structure all of this.

KLEBA: The problem is leaders think it's about having control. They should be thinking about influence. You can't work ON people. You have to work THROUGH them.

O'HARA: Are we saying what I think we're saying?

KLEBA: I can't believe I'm saying it but: yes. We have to become administrators.

O'HARA: We might forget what it's like to be teachers.

KLEBA: Good call. Just one of us then. Please let it be you.

O'HARA: Rock, paper, scissors?

          (They play. KLEBA wins.)

DR. O'HARA: Damn. OK.

          (Lights slowly fade.)

Don't get us wrong: we love administrators.

Hell, one of us is indeed an administrator and the other is a teacher who now also does PD for admin. We didn't write this book to be a takedown of "bad leadership" or some sort of sentimental or jokey rendering of the joys and miseries of school life. We wanted to make a practitioner's study of leadership from the shared vantage points of a teacher and an administrator. How is it that we'd never seen that before?

With close to 40 years of experience between us, we have a ground-level understanding of what happens in many schools. We've taught classes and taken classes. We've sat in on countless faculty meetings, Superintendent's Conference Days, and Back-to-School nights. Did we mention we hate lousy faculty meetings?

Whatever anyone can say about bad administrators—and there's a lot one can say— even the most cynical, charcoal-where-there-used-to-be-a-heart teachers have to admit that being in charge is hard.

We've seen what it's like to work for the greats and, hoo boy, it's night and day from working for a schlub. A great administrator is like a great professional coach or an amazing CEO: they build great teams and do great work no matter who they have working for them. A great administrator is like a chef in the family who can use regular, old ingredients in your fridge to make something sublime. They find the magic in the ordinary and can turn departments, schools, and sometimes whole districts into places where people want to be.

We wanted to write something that teachers AND administrators (and everybody else) might pick up and say, "Yeah, that's true." A kind of field manual that was irreverent yet earnest. Something real written by two people who are still doing the work under those strident tube lights and bell schedules in schools.

A lot of people inspired us, and you'll see their words as quotes at the beginning of each essay. We reference ideas from educational and organizational leadership research, pop culture, ancient texts, and Hollywood movies.

We believe that the most important work in the world is teaching. And no one is more important than administrators for the support and growth of teachers. We might not be able to fix the whole damn system, but we sure can make a lot of things better one administrator at a time. One teacher at a time. One student at a time.

And by that, we mean: you can.

We believe in you. A great leader can change the world through other people.

To paraphrase one of our heroes, Anthony Bourdain:

this one's for the teachers, and all those who have their backs.

> RWO and MJK,
> in a Starbucks in Jericho, Long Island, NY
> January 2020.

HOW TO USE
THIS BOOK

This is a handbook for those who have the wisdom, humor, and stamina to make the policy-ridden school machine operate as if people were human. Short and shareable, the essays can be read independently or in groups. For example, you can:

- take an essay and share it to spark authentic conversations with your teachers or colleagues.
- compare it against your own practice and see what resonates and what doesn't.
- use an essay when [fill in the crazy thing that happened at work today] kept you from planning something meaningful for the after-school meeting.
- use the book as a coaster for that much needed coffee.
- buy a thousand copies for your university teacher or administrator program.*
- give it as a gift to every member of your faculty* (along with chocolates or something–that's just good manners.)
  *We have incredibly competitive bulk rates.

How NOT to Use This Book

Like every bit of leadership advice ever written, some of this stuff will be useful to you and some of it won't. So, avoid the temptation to:

- make anyone read this–if they don't want to read it, they won't.
- make people see the same things in the essays that you see.

How This Book Is Organized

Otherful is...
broken into three parts we have discovered are the foundation of working with and leading humans.

1. **Natural Accountability:** recognizing that controlling others doesn't work
2. **The Conspiracy Ratio:** building and maintaining real relationships
3. **Contexting:** activating how you listen to help others understand things

   Stocked with short essays that end the same way:

   Otherful Principle: the big leadership idea
   Quick Skim: for when you want to read in a hurry
   Try This: some actions you can take right now
   Disclaimer: recognition that this work isn't easy and that there isn't just one way to do it

22 Quick Fixes to Create the School You Want is...

a practical guide for people who are leading schools right now.

   Even shorter explanations of things you deal with every day at school.
   Alphabetically listed for fast reference.

PART 1

NATURAL ACCOUNTABILITY

Natural Accountability
is the invisible hand
behind all motivation.

The people you lead have reasons for how they behave and what they say because they are first and always beholden to themselves. They are naturally accountable to the things that THEY care about and are concerned with just as you are to your cares and concerns.

Everyone's Natural Accountability is eternally at play whether you understand it or not.

Imposing your Artificial Accountability on them is counterproductive and impractical. You will not mandate their concern. You will only commandeer their time and erode their trust in you. If your people think you are in the way, you are ignoring their Natural Accountability.

Nobody wants to work hard and not get better. People want to do well and be recognized for their efforts. If you attend to what they care about, they'll seek your help.

You do not have to change anyone else. Your task is to help others to monitor and reflect on their own attempts to improve.

SIT UP STRAIGHT: AN INTRODUCTION TO NATURAL ACCOUNTABILITY

Dorothy: Oh, will you help me? Can you help me?
Glinda: You don't need to be helped any longer.
            You've always had the power to go back
            to Kansas.
Dorothy: I have?
Scarecrow: Then why didn't you tell her before?
Glinda: She wouldn't have believed me. She had
            to learn it for herself.

— *The Wizard of Oz*

F**k you. I won't do what you tell me.
—Rage Against the Machine

"Don't sit up straight," she said. "Inhibit and direct."

She'd been telling me to 'inhibit and direct' now for a few sessions. I was stuck on this first lesson. It wasn't easy. I knew if I were inhibiting and directing, I would be sitting up straight. But whenever I just sat up straight, she said, "No, don't just sit up straight. Inhibit and direct." I was tempted to think I was being had by this lovely young lady I visited twice a week during my senior year of college for Alexander Technique. But I was willing to be had. I wanted to impress her. I wanted to inhibit and direct. I just hadn't a clue how to do it.

Just sitting up straight, she explained, didn't alleviate the muscle stress caused by slouching. Instead, the stiffening of the back placed a second stress on the first stress. If one could instead inhibit the impulse to slouch and release the stress in the muscles that caused the slouching, then one could direct the shoulders upward, settling into the body's natural, stressless posture.

Consider the implications. Two people with what looks like good posture could have very different things happening in their backs:

1. "Sitting up Straight"—One could have a posture that is doubly stressed with muscles working against each other, creating a straight-looking posture but with increased stress on all of the muscles.

2. "Inhibiting and Directing"—One could have a posture that is natural and stress free.

Mandating Compliance vs. Offering Support

The same is true in school leadership. Two teams that appear to be working well could have very different things happening.

1. Artificial Accountability—The administrator sees the problems and tells the team of teachers how to solve them. Teachers must report their progress and are monitored/evaluated on how well they do what they're told.

2. Natural Accountability—The administrator empowers the team of teachers to see problems and determine solutions. The administrator monitors and coaches teachers in a constant process of trial, reflection, and improvement that builds teachers' capacity to monitor themselves.

The artificial accountability model is terribly inefficient because:

- **Classrooms belong to teachers**, just like the field belongs to athletes and the stage belongs to actors. Teachers are responsible for what happens in their classrooms and, therefore, must be in charge. A 180 day school year has a teacher running 600-900 lessons per year, making thousands of decisions every day. An admin sees maybe 2-5 of them. If you're a real hustler, you might see 1% of them. Every mandate from you that doesn't resonate with their natural accountability can destabilize their work and make you as a boss look clueless or, worse, overreaching.

- **Your "best practices" are yours—not theirs**. Your teachers have their best practices, too. Your practices might be great. They might have helped you change kids' lives when you were teaching. But here's the thing: you can't hand your Stradivarius to someone who doesn't play violin and expect beautiful music. Heck, they might be bassoonists. Or jugglers.

- **Teachers can either be responsive to their students or to you**. Which behavior do you think describes a better teacher and a better classroom?

- **No one likes being told what to do**. Including you.

The natural accountability model recognizes that the teachers are the game changers, the players on the field. They want to win just as much as you do. As a leader, you can help them help themselves. If you listen to teachers, you will hear about their achievements, goals, and challenges. If you listen, teachers will give you a blueprint for improvement efforts. Recognize the great things they are already doing. Ask how you can help them with what they are trying to do.

Teachers have enough stress. Don't add stress to stress. Inhibit your desire to change teachers and direct your efforts toward empowering teachers to change themselves. Your only other option is to double down on the artificial accountability model and blame the teachers when it doesn't work again. And we all have plenty of data on that model.

It's not simply about being a good, respectful leader. It's about being efficient and effective.

Right?

●THERFUL PRINCIPLE

External corrections are less effective
and shorter lasting than self corrections.

QUICK SKIM

Teachers already care and have reasons for doing what they do. When you tell teachers what to do rather than offer help as they figure out what to do themselves, you disrespect them and invite them to be inattentive to results. You make teachers feel inessential to their own work and then guess what: they believe you.

TRY THIS

Think about your own work for a moment.

- In your interactions with your teachers, what's your ratio of mandates vs. questions?

- How often is your thinking impacted by how a teacher describes something to you?

- Do you think that your teachers believe that they own their improvement efforts?

Make adjustments with this undeniable fact in mind: Teachers spend almost all of their time without you or your guidance.

Don't be distracted by the temptation to just tell people what to do. The more effective play is to help your teachers learn how to monitor and improve their own work. They need to work more for themselves than for you. Like students in a classroom, teachers need support, not control.

DISCLAIMER

Some teachers suck. So do some administrators. These are ugly truths. But, you know what? You only make things worse if you assume your teachers don't want to do good work. Given the two management systems, you'll grow much better teachers if you spend less time mandating and more time coaching. Believe your teachers can or cannot manage their own work—either way you'll be right. And you might be surprised: teachers often live up to the expectations from the boss.

EVERYONE IS ON FIRE

Motivation is the art of getting people to do what you want
them to do because they want to do it.
—Dwight D. Eisenhower

Those who hold conflicting frames pay attention
to different facts and make different sense
of the facts they notice.
—Donald Schon, *The Reflective Practitioner*

At night I wake up with the sheets soaking wet
And a freight train running through the middle
of my head...
—Bruce Springsteen, "I'm On Fire"

When the power goes out, which happens on occasion, I still flick the light switch when I go into another room.

It's a habit. When the lights don't come on, I remember the power is out and think again about how inconvenient it all is. My wife and I have some candles we light when we lose power—the same candles for the last 15 years; we don't have to use them often. Once there is nothing else to do, I watch the light from the candles flicker on the walls.

I have an ill-placed fireplace in my tiny dining room. I've never used it. I like watching a fire, but I don't want to have to deal with getting the chimney cleaned or moving the dinner table. Several of my friends have gotten fireplaces—all of them connected to a gas line.

It's easier. When you want a fire, you turn it on. When you are done, you shut it off. The fake wood inside them almost looks real.

Once upon a time, before powerlines brought electricity to every house, people needed fire all the time to warm and light their houses. We still use fire, but most of us don't interact with it directly. We expect the pilot light in the oil burner to be on by itself. When we want to fry eggs, we turn a dial and the fire comes on. We expect the power to light the LEDs. When it doesn't, we get frustrated.

The same is true of our interactions with people, particularly in hierarchies like those at school. Being in charge often means telling people what to do. We want to flick a switch and have people do what we want. When it doesn't work, we get frustrated, impatient, and sometimes insulted.

But here's the thing: your teachers and colleagues show up to school radiating the heat of their own lives. You can't light their fire. It's been lit long before they met you.

FIRE Moves Everyone

We invite you to use a lens we have developed in order to better recognize what's driving our teachers and colleagues at school. We call it FIRE. It's a way to replace judging what we think other people are doing with an attempt to understand what may be motivating them.

All people are driven by their

> F- Fears
> I- Interests
> R- Responsibilities, and
> E- Experiences.

You, too, can be understood this way. People's FIRE determines what they see and how they see it. When we don't realize this, we are bound for miscommunication with people whose FIRE lights up different things in different ways. Think of it this way: the people who make the most sense to you– whatever that means– are driven by FIRE that you can see and understand. Those whom you don't "get" are often driven by things you do not value or even acknowledge.

Until you see the FIRE in each of your people, you will have a hard time understanding what's going on within them. You'll also be hobbled in your ability to motivate or direct others if you don't know what's actually driving them already. Worse, if you don't understand your own FIRE, you won't even understand what's driving you. Until you see the FIRE in the room, you are powerless. Flick the switch all you want. The lights ain't comin' on.

Everyone's FIRE can be generative and destructive—and it cannot be extinguished. It's neither good nor bad, but it always is. You have to spend time studying your people and yourself. Humbly learn about people's FIRE so that you can serve them. Ignore their FIRE at your own peril. And as for your own FIRE: an unreflective leader can be a dangerous person in a school. But that isn't you, is it?

●THERFUL PRINCIPLE

People experience and respond to everything filtered through their fears, interests, responsibilities, and experiences.

◖UICK SKIM

People have reasons for their actions and words. All of us experience and respond to things through the filters of our fears, interests, responsibilities, and experiences (FIRE). A person's FIRE can help you achieve your goals for them at school—or it can scorch your relationship with them. As a leader at school, you should build much of your work around using and developing other people's FIRE.

Stop ignoring, battling, or trying to extinguish FIRE in others.

Instead of trying to shape the work of your teachers and colleagues, make it your goal to understand what motivates them. Put your efforts towards apprehending others' FIRE and then helping them harness it.

Your teachers want to do great work. Put the time in to learn what drives them. You'll get a much better sense of the variety of people who work for you and you'll have a much better chance of doing the greatest work of educational leadership: working through other people.

TRY THIS

- Study your people by looking for evidence of their fears, interests, responsibilities, and experiences. To do this well, you need to cultivate real relationships with them. Develop and maintain a genuine interest in your teachers and colleagues. Bring a humble curiosity to how and why they do what they do.

- Ask questions of your people and remember their answers. Notice your inclination to judge your people; instead, focus on what about another person's FIRE can be useful for school. Use those moments to study the limitations of your own FIRE.

- Remember: in education, it's usually much easier to develop a person than to sideline or replace them. We have to work with the people we have. To be that great leader who can work with anyone, you need to, well, work with anyone. That means not quitting on someone who bugs the heck out of you.

DISCLAIMER

Cute acronyms make the world worse. We know this. We didn't mean to make a cute acronym. But it just worked too well not to use. Check it out for yourself: next time you're listening to someone at work who drives you up the wall, look for his FIRE. Is this usually hard-to-understand person actually being powered by his fear? How about his interests? Responsibilities? Or is it his experience? Maybe he's not resisting YOU at all. It's amazing how much FIRE can illuminate a dark room of misunderstanding.

Dang. Did it again.

THE PARADOX OF PATTERNS

We see the world, not as it is, but as we are—or, as we
are conditioned to see it. When we open our mouths to
describe what we see, we in effect describe ourselves,
our perceptions, our paradigms.

—Steven R. Covey, *The 7 Habits of Highly Effective People*

In the beginner's mind there are many possibilities,
but in the expert's there are few.

—Shunryu Suzuki, *Zen Mind, Beginner's Mind*

People generally see what they look for,
and hear what they listen for.

—Harper Lee, *To Kill a Mockingbird*

There are no bored three year olds. They don't exist.

Three year olds want to know everything: they explore the
world through their eyes, with their hands, and with their whole
being. And that doesn't begin to describe a child in the presence
of a strong odor like fresh cookies or dog poo, or a loud sound like
fireworks or the garbage truck. The world is a whirling carousel of
curiosities to a child. Things shimmer with possibility and purpose.
Three year olds simply want to know everything.

So why don't twenty year olds? Or forty or fifty year olds, for
that matter?

Let's be blunt: why do so many teachers and administrators become incurious, close-minded professionals?

It likely has to do with the hidden cost of experience.

By the very nature of learning, we use our accumulated past experience to interpret our present experience. We feel both wise and safe when we recognize what's about to happen. We celebrate our ability to see the patterns in things; we tend to reward those with the most correct predictions. Our lives become safer and more stable as we become more steeped in the "causes and effects" of the world.

But something unfortunate happens as we continue to rely on our accumulated experience: our accurate predictions begin to erode our ability to experience something on its own terms. We experience fewer things that surprise us. If we dare to admit it, we have stopped looking.

This is the paradoxical cost to getting good at predicting patterns. We become close-minded, narrow-sighted observers without even knowing it. All of our hard fought wisdom transforms into a blindfold, cloaking the patterns we haven't seen before or simply don't recognize.

The Blindfold of Experience

When you observe your teachers, your experience is typically a great strength, but your inclination to look for patterns can blind and bind you. Because you are tasked with looking for problems, you can easily be pulled towards deficit patterns. You might look at your people and colleagues and think things like:

"She's a control freak"
"He's a mess"
"That lady hates kids"
"This guy is lazy as hell"

Nobody can blame you for this. Identifying these patterns in your teachers makes your interactions with them less complicated.

You are powerfully incentivized to see patterns quickly and, often, without much reflection. Let's face it, you have lots to do.

It begs the question: how often do you misread someone because of the pattern your experience has trained you to see? Check yourself: how much of a chance do any of your people have to change your mind about them?

As an educational leader, your opportunity to change your mind lies in seeing the growth potential of every teacher. The best among us respect the power of experience while leaving the door open for new experiences to alter the patterns. If you work in education, you must not simply believe in others' potential, you must also constantly look for and support this potential. Let's underline this. We are not talking about general optimism or positivity, though these are certainly good to have in your toolbox. We are talking about an intentional search for hidden abilities and underdeveloped gifts in your teachers and fellow leaders.

It is our mission as educators to develop and grow skills and talent. If we limit this mission merely to our students, we are creating a self-defeating hypocrisy where the children are encouraged to grow under teachers and colleagues who languish in the patterns that we have come to expect.

The Beginner's Mind

Be like a child when you observe your people.

Every time you are with them, attempt to see them as if you have never seen them before. During an observation, recognize your tendencies to judge and prejudge. Notice how often you want to "fix" or "improve" things. In meetings, be aware that how you are feeling that day (level of fatigue, state of mind, current life events) may put you in a place to find patterns that aren't even there. Put your biases in front of you, recognizing that your hard-won experience can be either helpful or distracting. Sometimes your experience can be your most dangerous ally.

It is a great paradox of leadership. Come to terms with the fact that the patterns you see so well can blind you to dozens of other patterns that have always eluded you. See where your expertise limits you so you can grow beyond it.

---

❶THERFUL PRINCIPLE

What you are looking for blinds you
to the things you aren't looking for.

QUICK SKIM

As you gain experience, your weaknesses can grow with your strengths. Patterns help us focus our attention. When we focus on something, we see it more deeply—but we also miss more. Notice the temptation to think your experience allows you to know your people better than they know themselves. Your beliefs about "how people learn" or "what makes a good teacher" are all potential blinders. Let your teachers constantly be the experts on who they are and what they do, and you will become the best thing a leader (or teacher) can be: a student to those you serve. Your people will teach you what they need.

And then, instead of leading the school that you think you have, you can lead the school you actually have.

TRY THIS

- Suspend your own thinking. When someone says or does something that runs against a pattern that you already have, and you're ready to interrupt them, catch yourself. Pause. You don't have to agree with your colleagues and your teachers. But you'll be a much better leader if you've done the hard work to listen and watch them without judgment. You can't understand them if you're paying more attention to your own ideas and patterns rather than listening and learning from theirs.

- Take responsibility for your biases. Create a list of what you look for in your teachers. You, like everyone, have a few patterns that jump out at you. You are biased to see these patterns in your teachers and colleagues (and in your real life, too). You don't always misidentify them, but when you do you are as dangerous as glass on the beach. How many of your people have you misunderstood? Answer: not zero.

- What you don't see in your people is more relevant than what you do see. Your vision will always be incomplete. Because of this, every prescription you give them has the potential to be a proof point to them that you don't actually know them or don't know what you're talking about. Be humble. All of your teachers know things that you haven't even considered. Don't invite their derision because you disrespect that.

- Practice listening for what's there instead of what you think is there.

DISCLAIMER

We don't think three-year-olds would manage the joint better than you do. Your treasure trove of experiences is the foundation of your expertise. It might be that your experiences are, in fact, an amazing blueprint of everything you have ever seen at school. But blindspots have a way of embedding themselves. The great paradox of sight and blindness has challenged leaders since the dawn of civilization. There's a reason why blind prophets appear in ancient stories from around the globe. Your vision as a leader may be on

point most of the time, but the wisest know: no one can see everything.

HOW I LOST US
THE WORLD SERIES

Don Draper: That's your job. I give you money;
                    you give me ideas.
Peggy Olson: And you never say, "thank you."
Don Draper: That's what the money is for!

—Mad Men, Season 4, Episode 7

And why beholdest thou the splinter that is in thy
brother's eye, but considerest not the wooden beam
that is in thine own eye?

—Matthew 7:3

You probably think this song is about you.

—Carly Simon, "You're So Vain"

I was in a bar in Baton Rouge watching all-star pitcher Mariano
Rivera walk into the final inning of the seventh and final game of
the 2001 World Series.

The Yankees had lost the first two games of the series before
winning the next three. Then they lost the sixth game and needed
to win this seventh game. The game was scoreless for the first five
innings before the Diamondbacks scored a run in the sixth inning.
The Yankees followed up with a run in the seventh and the eighth.

They were up two to one. And then they brought in Rivera, the legendary closer. Rivera was so good that he's the first player in baseball history to be inducted into the Hall of Fame unanimously on the first vote. He was so good, his nickname was "The Sandman" for his ability to put other teams "to sleep." He was a killer– the best in the game. As far as I was concerned the game was over.

At the time, I'd been away, acting in a national tour of the 18th Century French comedy classic and barnburner, *Tartuffe*. (Aside: I worked as a professional actor for a year– and learned more than a few skills that will be useful for the next professional development session I'll be hosting at your school). I missed home, particularly in the months following 9/11. During the ninth inning, I called my dad to rejoice in the Yankees' win. He couldn't believe I called to celebrate a win before the game was over. He rushed me off the phone right before Rivera gave up a couple of runs. My dad still blames me for the Yankees' loss.

And he's not alone. I know many people who have game watching rituals that they believe impact the outcome of the game they are watching. If pushed, most would laugh about the idea that the color of the socks they wear impacts the outcome of a game they are watching. Some probably really believe it. That so many people come to entertain, if even just for fun, this idea–that they themselves impact a game they have nothing to do with–reminds us that when we are not paying attention, most of us engage with the universe as if we are the center of it.

This default belief is the root of so many of our problems.

Seeing ourselves as the center of the universe doesn't only make us selfish, it leads us to see our world and everyone in it as for us or against us. It leads us to see people's actions as a referendum on us. They don't just do things–they do things to me.

Everybody is In My Way

Living on Long Island, I spend a lot of time in traffic. I have found myself frustrated by people who have gotten into car accidents because it caused me to be stuck in traffic. "Why are they so careless," I think. "Don't they see they are holding everyone up?" And I still think this after losing my brother to a traffic accident. My mind still goes there. I find myself wishing that the people in the other cars around me didn't exist so that I could get where I'm going a little faster.

Our default sense of ourselves as the center of the universe is insidious. And it's even worse when we are in positions of power.

We are already inclined to see people and their actions in terms of how they impact us. When we become the boss, we become even less likely to question this inclination. Rather than see someone else's perspective, we think, "Well, this is what they're getting paid for. They don't have to like their job; they just have to do it." Failure to communicate is THEIR fault. And as long as it's their fault, we have no need to change ourselves.

Unchecked, this sense can lead us to see our colleagues, particularly our subordinates (subordinates, think about that for a second), as prostitutes, bums, and criminals. We stop caring about how they feel about the initiative. We just want them to do it. When they don't do it, we lament their laziness or shortcomings. We might begin to wonder what those teachers might try to "get away with" if we aren't watching.

The truth is: almost nothing that happens anywhere is about you. Even in your most intimate relationships, those you hold closest are doing little that is about you. Slow down. There are so many factors that impact why things happen and whether or not they are "good" outcomes. Every time we think it's mostly about us and how we see things, we miss all the other things that other people are actually doing.

When the Yankees lost, my dad blamed me. But a few of the cheering fans in that bar in Baton Rouge, delighted that I single-handedly brought the mighty Yankees to their knees with a call to my father, bought me a drink.

OTHERFUL PRINCIPLE

When we think it's all about us, we misinterpret
and judge others' actions.

QUICK SKIM

You are not the center of anyone else's world, no matter what
the title is on your desk or your door, Big Shot. Our default sense
of ourselves as the center of the universe causes us to incriminate
others. Seeing people as obstacles or perpetrators undermines our
ability to lead them.

TRY THIS

- Beware! You are constantly judging everyone who works for
  you. You can't turn it off and you never will. This isn't bad,
  inherently– but it is dangerous.

- Question yourself relentlessly. Am I helping others? Or am
  I just judging how I think someone is impacting me or my
  goals? Do I keep evaluating others basically on how much
  they do or don't agree with my view of the world?

- When you take something personally at work, instead of
  reacting, see it as a red flag. You might be about to make a
  poor decision instead of learning something.

DISCLAIMER

Nope, not on this one. You are not the center of the universe.

LETHAL WEAPON

[Fezziwig] has the power to render us happy or unhappy;
to make our service light or burdensome; a pleasure or a toil.
Say that his power lies in words and looks; in things so
slight and insignificant that it is impossible to add and
count 'em up: what then? The happiness he gives, is quite
as great as if it cost a fortune.
—Charles Dickens, *A Christmas Carol*

Nobody is as powerful as we make them out to be.
—Alice Walker

Joey Roma, like many of our school security guards, was a former
NYPD police officer.

He was posted at a desk by the main entrance to keep the school
secure from threats. He also kept the traffic circle in front of the
school moving, and he let people know when they were holding
things up—he didn't mince words. I never saw him eat. That has
nothing to do with this essay, but I worked with him for 10 years
and never saw him eat. I suppose, if nothing else, it just adds to his
Homeric character.

Joey never had to secure the school against an attack, but as far
as the teachers were concerned, he provided security all the time.
When district administration visited the school, he did everything
short of playing the Star Wars Imperial March over the loudspeak-

ers. Before automated texts, phone calls, and emails, we had a phone chain to let teachers know when there was a snow day. Joey had helped teachers create their own phone chain to let them know when district administration visited the school, and he was the First Responder.

The funny thing is most of the teachers were great. They should have been thrilled at the chance to strut their stuff. But, they were as thankful for the chain as teachers who weren't great. When I found out about it, I asked Joey why teachers were so concerned about the visits. He asked if I'd ever heard of anything good coming from district administration visiting a classroom. I hadn't. Then Joey asked if I'd ever heard of anything bad coming from district administration visiting a classroom. I had.

I wonder if the district administrators had a clue that this was happening. When they did enter classrooms, teachers smiled and welcomed them as if they were grateful for the visit. And as soon as the admin left the building, teachers would find out which rooms they'd been in and if everything was OK.

I am a district administrator now.

After I visit schools, teachers talk to each other to find out which rooms I visited and if everything was OK. I have realized how hard it is to make teachers feel like something good has happened as a result of my visiting their classes and how easy it is to make them feel like something bad has happened. I have realized that teachers' fears have little to do with my intentions.

All Power Can Be Threatening

Let's acknowledge an easily overlooked and sometimes uncomfortable truth about the dynamic between teachers and administrators. There is an undeniable chasm between these lanes that only a few professionals can bridge (and this almost always through personal friendship). Simply, admin and teachers don't–and often can't–spend much time together.

Many administrators see little of a teacher's actual work in the classroom. To make sense of what that teacher is doing, an admin must build a projection from a few precious snapshots. So, nearly any moment an admin walks into a classroom (formally or informally) can become THE example of the entirety of that teacher's practice.

Everything in an interaction between an admin and teacher can become heightened, a forensic exercise in which the teacher may worry that every word or action may be captured and analyzed. Hyper-awareness of every imperfection—of which there will be many because nobody is perfect—becomes exhausting and uncomfortable. And all of this gets further complicated as the teacher has to attend to what different administrators prioritize because they don't all prioritize the same thing.

Even if the admin notes some good things, the teacher will wonder if the admin also noticed the imperfections. "Is my admin being entirely honest? Or might she be holding back what she thinks of me?"

Inevitably, because everyone is human, moments will be overlooked or misunderstood. No matter how well one interaction or observation can go, an intangible fear may persist.

Kindness Isn't Weakness

If you were a teacher, do you remember this feeling? Can you connect it to how you might feel when interacting with higher ups who observe or evaluate your work now? And all of us feel the pressure to be perfect in front of our students' parents. Heck, you might avoid eating at some restaurants in your district for the same reason. It's not out of fear that you'd be bothered but, rather, that someone might judge you on how you behave, what you eat or drink, or who's in your company.

You have the ability to use your dangerous power the way you choose. You cannot become un-dangerous and shouldn't even try. But you can be careful to respect that your people's fear isn't unreasonable or without burdens to them. Kindness from the person with lethal power can become even more impactful. A smile from Fezziwig was a ray of sunlight for Ebeneezer Scrooge. And Scrooge's eventual smile, in turn, became the warmth that saved Tiny Tim.

●THERFUL PRINCIPLE

Remember that the boss makes people nervous.

●UICK SKIM

Make no mistake—your title makes you like an occupying force. It doesn't matter that you are there to do good. Go ahead, hand out candy bars to the kids—it doesn't stop your people from fixing their eyes on your weapons, body armor, and night vision goggles. Every threatening gesture you make, intentional or not, goes into the public record of how your people think and feel about you. You can undo the years of carefully built trust and relationships in one moment.

TRY THIS

• Be aware that your people are always worried when you come around. Make it a goal to pay attention to and address this when you can.

• Your power not only amplifies how dangerous you can be; it amplifies your power as an ally, as well. You can use your power to aid your people, by defending them or getting them help when they are in trouble.

• And, for heaven's sake, don't put your hands anywhere near your weapons unless you are going to use them. Don't even think lightly (or joke with an administrative colleague) about changing a teacher's schedule or any other sanction. You may not realize it, but your people are watching you as if they are at a gun fight at high noon.

DISCLAIMER

You can't do your job and not be dangerous to your people. Attempts to be the "un-scary" boss will ultimately invite derision from some of your people (who'll see you as soft or inattentive) or suspicion from some of those you report to (who'll see you as spineless or lazy). You ARE dangerous—and you need to be. Our students and schools need to be protected from those who would perform bad, illicit, and/or harmful behavior. It's one of your greatest challenges: your lethality must be rare and precise. And it will never not be a burden to you.

THE GODFATHER

Creon:	I want to save you, Antigone.
Antigone:	You are the king, and you are all powerful. But that you cannot do.
Creon:	You think not?
Antigone:	Only this can you do: have me put to death.
Creon:	Should I have you tortured, perhaps?
Antigone:	Why should you do that? To see me cry? To hear me beg for mercy? Or swear whatever you wish, and then begin over again?

—Jean Anouilh's *Antigone*

I'm going to make him an offer he can't refuse.

Vito Corleone, *The Godfather*

So what if he got shot a bunch of times? The Godfather survived, at least for a while.

When his eldest son gets murdered, his youngest avenges his brother's death. The Godfather doesn't miss his chance to get sweet revenge, too. He orders assassinations and vendettas. He arranges for enemies to wake to their prized horses' heads in their beds. He gets his way—until he doesn't.

"I'm gonna make him an offer he can't refuse" is listed by the American Film Institute as the second greatest movie quote of all time. According to an article in Forbes, *The Godfather* ranks as many CEO's most loved movie. The movie is a cultural touchstone because it distills a truth of our existence: each of us, left to our own devices, wants things our way, regardless of how others feel.

For a while, the Godfather lives like a king. He is the big man in charge. He lays waste to his enemies and sips espresso made for him by his butler. But while there are a few who love him, many more hate him. He survives a few assassination attempts and dies of a heart attack in his garden, chased by those who would kill and replace him.

And yet, what a way to go, right? That's how a leader does it! The style! The power!

The Godfather is like a box of cigarettes to a smoker. The warnings are right there on the box, but we can't resist it.

Sometimes You Have to Twist a Few Arms

With enough force, you can have your way for a while.

When we want to channel our inner Vito Corleone, we are not looking to fail; we are looking to win. It's when we want to win hard with the loudmouth at work who never shuts up or the boss who doesn't appreciate us or the pain-in-the-ass customer who never stops haggling or the neighbor who is always having loud parties or the parents who never listen or the kids who never listen or the spouse who never listens. We just want to win. And if we could just make them an offer they couldn't refuse, if we could just shut them up, then we could breathe, we could relax, we could stop trying to convince/beg/placate/bribe them. It would feel so good to show them who's boss.

If only it were that easy. It's not.

Sometimes telling people what to do works for a while. But, in the end, it usually does more harm than good–just like the last time that you were told that you had to do something against your will. Remember that? That went over real big, right? Too often, we can lose sight of what we actually want; we let our egos get in the way. We don't just want to win, we want to exert our power over the less powerful. We want to strut. We get offended by those we lead when they don't fall into step.

And when we force them to do something they don't want to do, we trade a short term win for a long term cost.

It's My Job To Be In Charge

You risk more than losing a potential ally when you make people simply execute your commands; you risk losing people's confidence in you. People pay attention to those in power. When an administrator forces somebody to do something, other teachers begin to wonder if and when they'll be next. They don't know if they can trust the leader. The shame is that the directive probably won't help you get what you were hoping for from that person anyway, and it might ruin your relationship with others.

The problem is when you need people to do something, you need THEM. And when you need someone, the worst thing you can do is make that person feel coerced or humiliated. You don't want to feel that way and neither does anyone else. Don't fall into the trap of taking the momentary win and the high of getting your way only to find later that you've made an enemy out of a potential ally.

It's amazing how often people high up the hierarchy just assume that people will get in line once a decision is made. These leaders rarely see themselves as being violent or demanding. They are just doing the job of making decisions, they often think. But schools are funny places. The people who make the decisions are rarely the ones who are executing them. Just expecting people to do what they're told can have a disastrous impact on morale.

People might put up with you for a while, but not for long. But don't take our word for it. Take the American Film Institute's. Do you know what movie quote beat Corleone's command for the best quote of all time?

"Frankly, my dear, I don't give a damn."

OTHERFUL PRINCIPLE

You can't make anyone do anything.
In schools, especially, coercion doesn't work.

QUICK SKIM

One of the greatest leadership fantasies is that the boss gets to tell others what to do. This is connected to another leadership fantasy: the higher you ascend the hierarchy, the easier it is to get other people to do things. These fantasies distract us from an undeniable truth: we cannot make anyone do anything. Leaders don't coerce—thugs do. And you know what thugs can't do? Lead.

TRY THIS

• When you become a school leader, you have to leave behind the personal disputes, the ultimatums, and the temptation to prove your strength to would be challengers. Give up the idea that you have the power or the right to make anyone do what you want.

• Practice asking for help in doing what you want, even though you don't have to. Instead of a directive, try saying "I have an idea for something and I need your help." Your teachers are pros. Instead of asking for fealty, ask for their assistance. It's an incredibly powerful move if it's done honestly and humbly.

• Hold yourself to a higher standard than you hold your people. Your title and salary don't mean anyone serves you. In fact, it basically means the opposite.

DISCLAIMER

It's not that you won't ever have to take action against one of your people. Attend to whatever your job requires of you, even the unpleasant stuff like firing, transferring, or disciplining people. Just don't do it because of your ego.

LE BIG MAC

But he tried to make the cider house rules seem friendly.
He phrased the rules in a confiding voice...
But every year, the piece of paper itself would
become worn and tattered
and used for other things - a kind of desperation grocery list,
for example, always by someone who couldn't spell...
At times, the solitary sheet of paper gathered little insults
and mockeries of a semi-literate nature.

—John Irving, *The Cider House Rules*

Educational policies must be designed as a shell within which
the kernel of professional judgment and decision making
can function comfortably.

—Lee S. Shulman, *The Wisdom of Practice*

Experience will guide us to the rules.
You cannot make rules precede practical experience.

—Antoine de Saint-Exupéry

I like Big Macs. My wife wants me to like them less.

So, I rarely have them now. When I do order a Big Mac, though,
I know what to expect—right down to the placement of the pickles.
Big Mac construction is precise and endlessly replicable. McDonald's is known the world over for policy and standardization. You

can get the same burgers and fries on six continents. McDonald's franchises use the same ingredients, the same machines for preparation, the same process for sandwich construction. There are no variables when making a Big Mac. I know because I used to make them when I worked at McDonald's when I was in high school. I didn't have to make decisions. I just followed the process I'd been taught, and it worked every time. I knew what I was seeking to achieve and that never changed. I always made a Big Mac the same way.

Everyone in education knows: teachers and students are not Big Macs. It's obvious that using the same strategies for attending to people that we use for attending to Big Macs is stupid. But that doesn't seem to keep us in schools from writing and using "Big Mac Rules."

People are complex; they bring varied talents and challenges. Teachers, especially, must be complex in order to do the job they do. It's a fundamental error to seek to make each person the same— whether we are talking about teachers or students. One size does not fit all. What works for some will not work for others.

The Rules Don't Run the School; Professionals Do

Big Mac Rules seriously endanger professional practice. The manager at Mickey D's doesn't want a kid on the burger line to interpret the onion-to-mustard ratio—just make the damn burger, he says to himself (and to the kid). But the principal of the school, overseeing that teacher who has the future salutatorian in the same class as a kid who lost her mother in October, desperately relies on the teacher to interpret situations and make a thousand context-specific decisions.

Directives like these tell teachers that no one trusts them or their judgment. They remove the teacher from the consequences of decision-making because the teachers don't make the decisions, the rules do.

Examples of "Big Mac Rules" that you should avoid as much as you can:

1. Rules meant to catch lousy teachers/administrators
   "Every teacher must post a 'Do Now' on the board for every lesson."

2. Rules meant to make administrators feel like they're in control of things they are actually not in control of
   "All teachers must submit weekly lesson plans to their supervisor."

3. Rules that everyone hates, complains about, and/or works around
   "This door is not to be used as an exit" (above the door that everyone uses as an exit).

As an administrator, how you manage your teachers is your most important job. The balance you strike between administering rules and preserving professional judgment is mission critical. If you are preparing to issue a rule made for teachers you wished you didn't have to deal with, proceed with caution: you might be making a Big Mac Rule.

Don't give your people a reason to believe you doubt their ability to make good decisions. Because they'll believe you.

⬤THERFUL PRINCIPLE

Rules are not a substitute for professional judgment.

⬤UICK SKIM

Teachers are not one size fits all—never forget this at school.

Context matters. Creating rules to override practitioners' judgment discourages people from using their judgment. And good teacher judgment is good for the whole school, especially the kids (and you, for that matter).

TRY THIS

- Before you make a rule, think about why you need it. Before you cite a rule as a reason for requiring someone to do something, think about how parents sound when they say, "because I said so."

- Identify any rule that overrides anyone needing to use professional judgment. Should you keep enforcing it? It might be one of those rare rules people should actually just shut up and follow. But every single one of those rules can invite your people to believe that you don't trust their professionalism.

- Get used to saying to your teachers: Trust yourselves. Just do what you think is the right thing every time. When we make a mistake, we'll learn from it.

DISCLAIMER

We are not saying that you shouldn't have any rules. Rules are essential and undergird all school systems. What we are saying is that most organizations have many more rules than are necessary. Rules can conflict with one another. They can have unintended consequences. They can make more sense to the person that made them than to the people that must abide by them. And they might be administered by those who seek to cover themselves and to skip the trouble of actually working with teachers.

PART 2

THE CONSPIRACY RATIO

The Conspiracy Ratio
is the inescapable reality that
the more the work belongs to you,
the less it can belong to anyone else.

To lead your people, you must first recognize that they live and work in their world, not yours. They need to own their work. (And frankly, you don't have time to do everyone else's job.)

Because your teachers are the experts and leaders of what's happening in their rooms, it is your essential task to learn who they are and what they care about. They don't "buy in" to you—it's the other way around.

"Conspiracy" comes from the Latin:

con- *"with"*

spirare- *"to breathe"*

It's what strong teams and communities do together.

Your people cannot require you to step out of your office—you have to choose to do that. And until you spend time with them in their worlds, breathing their air, you have very little capacity to actually support them.

While in your people's world, you must resist your desire to control things you do not control and, instead, help others to own what they own— and then empower them to lead it. Your place in the hierarchy gives you the power to bless their autonomy and ownership.

You'll earn their trust if you're around, not trying to change them. And that gives you the chance to influence them.

And influence trumps control every time.

WE DID IT MY WAY: AN INTRODUCTION TO THE CONSPIRACY RATIO

> The only thing you can really control
> is how you react to things out of your control.
>
> —Bassam Tarazi

> People don't resist change. They resist being changed.
>
> —Peter Senge's *The Fifth Discipline*

> It is amazing what you can accomplish if you do not care who
> gets the credit.
>
> —Harry S. Truman

You know how there are some teachers who are just plain lousy at classroom management?

Or how some other teachers tend to have the same battles with kids and/or parents year after year? It might not be cool or politically advantageous to say it out loud, but we all know a few teachers who have trouble holding it down.

When you listen to these teachers talk about it, they usually say something like: "That boy is disrespectful to everyone. I'm not going to accept that kind of behavior." Or…"it's an unusually bad group this year. None of these students ever want to do any work!"

Or…"I don't understand why these kids act this way. That group of girls causes havoc in every class. They don't listen!"

What is it that these teachers don't understand?

Simply, teachers who try to control their students tend to fail. Teachers who constantly demand respect rarely get it. Teachers who attempt to be at the center of importance forget that a well-run class is animated by the students, not the teacher.

It's more common than we probably want to admit. Even your great teachers sometimes forget that school isn't about them.

And so it goes with administrators, too.

The Cold, Hard Truth About Control

Control and influence are not the same thing, although they are often confused.

- **Control** creates an economy by employing punishments and/or incentives. Control works ON or OVER others.
- **Influence** creates a climate by inspiring, ennobling, and equipping others. Influence works THROUGH others.

Influence is a conspiracy relationship, a trust in "Us." Influence is about "We"- we're in this together. Because its dynamics depend on the followers' investment in that relationship, the chief goal of an influencer is to secure and maintain trust.

If your people don't truly believe in whatever initiative, system, or change you are leading, the minute you turn around they will do very little to help make it work.

It might be hard to accept, but you are one of the least important, "most important" people in your whole school community. Imagine this for a moment: if both you and a custodian didn't show up to work for a whole week, only one of you would be truly missed by the community. Can you guess which one?

You can point in the direction you want people to go, tell them what words and methods to use. But if they don't want to do it, your people are forced into a terrible choice: they can become puppets, rebels, or dropouts. None of those options make for good collaborators.

It's a cold, hard truth about control but usually, the harder you try to get your way, the less you will.

Your Greatest Power Rests In Other People

There's something ancient at work here that deserves your attention. It is an inversely proportional dynamic that we call the "Conspiracy Ratio."

<table>
<tr><td>The MORE
it's about you</td><td>:</td><td>The LESS it can
be about those you
are trying to lead</td></tr>
</table>

Naturally, the opposite is also true—and preferable.

Let's be clear. This is not about being unselfish or generous. It's a simple understanding that the more you row the boat, the less your team can. And the less they can, the less they will.

It's just like those teachers who think class is all about them.

When administrators think of themselves as the vending machine of the "What" and the "How," they immediately begin hindering the progress of others to develop. They begin crowding out their own people's ability to be invested. People cannot be invested in something that does not belong to them.

Your goal must be to gain influence, not control.

If you want to empower your people, you have to share your power.

OTHERFUL PRINCIPLE

The more it's about you, the less it can be
about those you are trying to lead.

QUICK SKIM

As a leader at school, you can't do anything by yourself. When you collaborate with others, and you're higher up in the pecking order, you have a tremendous opportunity to create a culture of responsibility and shared ownership. But to do it, you must give some of your power away. Most of us don't want to do this. It can leave us feeling vulnerable in the short term— but it is the only way to earn great influence in the long term. Don't unwittingly force your teachers to become puppets, rebels, or dropouts. You can't work ON your teachers. You can only work THROUGH them.

TRY THIS

- Identify your temptation to be in control of things you cannot control. Do your best to master it.

- Recognize that your teachers need to own what they do. Make it your mission to let go of your dreams of what you think that should look like.

- Build faculty meetings around what the teachers want, not what you want. This includes Superintendent's Conference Day. Why not take one of them and rename it "Teachers' Conference Day?" And let them do whatever they want with it.

- Be open to being overruled by those you rule.

- Change course when you get useful feedback. And if you aren't getting useful feedback, then that's because people don't believe you are really asking for it.

DISCLAIMER

Sometimes you have to be the boss. Sometimes you need to rule with an iron fist. Sometimes your teachers and colleagues are actually wrong and you are actually right. Just be careful. All the world's Pharaohs and most of its Kings are gone, but teachers are still doing their work in every country and culture on the planet.

EVERY SCHOOL IS
SKI SCHOOL

When we avoid taking risks and trying new things,
we can expect that same unwillingness from others.
"Leading" often means going first.

—George Couros, *The Innovator's Mindset*

Vulnerability is the birthplace of connection and the path to
the feeling of worthiness. If it doesn't feel vulnerable, the
sharing is probably not constructive.

—Brené Brown

The wound is where the light comes in.

-Rumi

On a winter's day when I was 9 years old, my mom surprised us with a wild idea.

"I need you to find your warmest gloves and hats in the box by the door," she told me and my two younger sisters. "When you find them, stuff them into the pockets of your winter jackets. You're going to need them bright and smearly tomorrow." Mom intentionally screwed up the pronunciation of words to crack us up.

Excited, we scrambled to the box in the laundry room and began rummaging through our winter clothing, tossing singleton mittens and gloves in the air.

"What are we doing?" my sister Kate yelled to my mom. Kate was the smart one. Sarah and I were just up for the adventure of looking for hats, blissfully unaware of what we were going to do the next day. Mom poked her head through the door.

"We're going skiing," she said, a twinkle in her eye. "You're going to meet Gunther."

Growing up in a suburb outside of Philadelphia, there was only one slope to go to- the infamous Spring Mountain- a hill so small we called it "The Bump." Gunther was the famous general manager of the joint and ran the ski school. He was an old mountaineer from Austria, his wrinkled face weathered from years in the Alps, a brush of hair grey at the temples. I remember his red jacket, his rare smile, and the clever way he taught us how to ski.

"You have to learn to fall!" he screamed in his first lesson, and every lesson after that. "It is the basis of all skiing!" Gunther yelled all the time. "Learning to fall will become your secret power! You will learn to be a skier of courage and grace when you always know how to fall!"

He showed us how to bend our knees and turn our skis perpendicular to the slope, softening the fall with our hips. He showed us how to relax when we'd go down, warning us of the dangers of stiffening up or bracing.

"I have fallen hundreds of times! I fell during a race once! On TV! I fell in front of my wife the first time we met! Falling is the most important part of learning how to ski!"

We didn't know if he was telling the truth, and we didn't care. Gunther gave us room to find our confidence. He helped us trust ourselves, like we were some sort of junior elite ski team learning insider tricks from a World Master.

Gunther helped us be strong for ourselves. I still hear his voice in my head when I think about how important it is that we learn how to fall.

The Real "F-word" In School

In my school hangs a banner that says "You learn nothing from success! Failure is the BEST teacher!"

I'm not sure I buy it. In a world of competitive test scores, high stakes observations, and viral news stories about school failures, do we really believe that failure–or falling of any kind–is good?

My experience is that many of us in the education profession see every error as a potential major blunder that can derail a school year or career. The ugly truth is that many people who work in school live in fear, covering up mistakes or doing everything they can to avoid risk. Our job is to look perfect.

What would Gunther think about how you are leading your school or department? Have you fallen hundreds of times? Do you know HOW to fall (graciously and without serious injury?) Do your people feel safe falling in front of you and in front of each other?

We invite you to ask yourself a few questions:

- How much do the teachers or other administrators at your school really know about you?

- Do they know just how bad you were when you first started teaching?

- Have they heard about the time you probably should have lost your job because of that dumb thing you said to a student or parent?

- How about that time you forgot about a deadline and had to go through massive heroics to cover up how much of a mess you made?

- Do they know that you worry about failing? Or falling?

If you want to change the hard-to-change, to move a school community in a new direction, you are going to have to take off that armor. Or, at least a part of it. Be assured, they won't take off theirs until you take off yours– and how are you going to get anything done with a bunch of scared folks walking around in heavy armor?

As a leader in your school, you are a model. What you do becomes an example. People will be vulnerable if you are vulnerable; they will be guarded if you are guarded. When you are brave and willing to fall in front of them, they will be brave and willing to fall. This is your secret power.

●THERFUL PRINCIPLE

The myth of the perfect, flawless boss is bad for everyone— including the boss.

●UICK SKIM

A great leader walks the walk. You want to make people trustworthy? You have to trust them. Take off the armor sometimes. Sharing your flaws with the people who work for you is the only way to encourage real risk taking. You want innovation and resilience? Let your people see your errors. People do not feel safe around someone who never shares a mistake.

TRY THIS

Publicly acknowledge your vulnerability.
- In a 1:1 or group setting, acknowledge that you simply don't know something or that you messed up in some way. Laugh about it or apologize as appropriate. Then carry on. They'll notice.

- When you need to confer with colleagues about their mistakes, tell a brief story about one of your own mistakes. Include what you learned and how you recovered. They might spread the word.

- Keep an eye on the temptation to minimize (or ignore) your own errors in real time. In a meeting, when your skis go flying out from under you, admit it and get back on your feet! It might be awkward. You might let a few people down—especially if they are in love with the idea of perfection. But grace doesn't come from sticking the landing; it comes from the willingness to be a humble learner in front of an audience. It might be one of the most powerful things you can do for your people.

DISCLAIMER

Sometimes it's going to hurt when we fall. Sometimes we can't show that we failed. It's true. The boss needs to look tougher than the rest of us. People want to follow a courageous warrior and there will be times when you will be sure you are anything but. So here's maybe the greatest contradiction we share in this whole collection: sometimes you have to fake it. Sometimes you need to pretend that everything is fine even though it isn't. There's no manual on when you need to show them that stiff upper lip, but we imagine you'll know.

THE MARATHON FAN

Be not afraid of greatness.
Some are born great, some achieve greatness,
and some have greatness thrust upon them.

—William Shakespeare, *Twelfth Night*

Emily: I didn't realize. So all that was going on and we never noticed... Do any human beings ever realize life while they live it?—every, every minute?

Stage Manager: No. (Pause.) The saints and poets, maybe—they do some.

—Thornton Wilder, *Our Town*

If you believe in them and give them an opportunity to perform, then they believe in themselves.

—Esther Wojcicki

Something strange and magical happens to you when you witness a marathon in person.

I remember my first time watching the New York City marathon. I was standing near a bodega in Williamsburg, waiting for a friend to pass. Hordes of runners that I didn't know and would never see again were lumbering by, numbered and panting. Meanwhile, people like me, standing in our pathetic jeans and scarves sipping our Starbucks, were there to just watch them strive.

Those humans flying by were not running away from danger nor running towards tacos: they were just running. Running to run. These were everyday people doing something extraordinary and difficult and amazing.

If you've ever watched a marathon in person, then you know. Watching a marathon isn't like watching football or basketball; cheering for a single person, even for a moment, can feel personal and intimate. It's rather easy to begin to truly care for the runners. You clap for complete strangers, people that you will never see again, hoping to transfer some of your energy to them to help them finish. You think: these people are heroes! You make eye contact with one of them and you automatically yell, "You got this!" In that moment, they're not just running for themselves. They're running for you, for the people standing next to you, for everyone—for all humans everywhere, ever. And as you cheer for them, you feel like you are cheering for the best in all of us.

I've come to find that almost everyone who has ever watched a marathon in person ends up feeling this for at least a moment or two. It's not weird to see spectators with tears in their eyes. It's testimony to the profound sense of awe in the face of other humans' magnificence.

When Leaders Are In Awe of Their People

This is how great teachers see their students—and it's how great administrators see their teachers. Great leaders traffic in the greatness of OTHER people. They look for it in the people around them—and, because they look for it, they find it.

As a school leader, it's tempting—hell, it can be fun—to fantasize about hiring fresh runners for the race of education at your school. Some of your teachers are just plain tired and set in their ways. "If I just had some people with fresh legs and open minds, I could make this school really WORK," you might imagine.

But that's the trap.

You are all running a marathon every day. You ever notice that everyone is tired at school most of the time? As the leader, your job is to help people find those wells of strength that you know they've trained for but that your people doubt they have.

Their Biggest Fan

Probably your most pivotal job as a school leader is to attract, inspire, develop, and maintain great educators. Point to a school that is really doing great work—truly kicking butt and changing students' lives—and you will likely find at least one leader who is simply in awe of her educators.

Sure, she loves the students. But she bleeds for her teachers and staff.

She runs alongside them when they're innovating a new practice; she reminds them of their forgotten efforts and unsung wins. She's their biggest fan. And there she is at mile 18, standing next to a table covered with cups of water that she set up with her own hands. She has proud tears streaming down her face and her throat is hoarse from yelling "YOU GOT THIS!" Her job is to be a super fan of her people and, by golly, they all know it.

You have to marry that faith in your teachers' and administrators' greatness with a desire to honestly see it and support it, and you gotta let 'em know, over and over.

If (more like when) you ever feel like YOU are losing your mojo, take another look at those magnificent humans who teach at your school. Bask in the authenticity and earnest work of their struggle to work with the students. They're staying up late and coming in early, helping younger humans find themselves. Handling crazy stuff that no one even sees. Those people are doing the most important job in humanity next to parenting. They're amazing.

And they're worth the very best (and as many cheers as) you've got.

OTHERFUL PRINCIPLE

Look for the greatness in your people and you will help them find it.

QUICK SKIM

All of the people who report to you at school are as amazing as every student they teach. Be open to being in awe of your teachers. Pay attention to those little details that reveal how unique and talented your people are. Open yourself to how hard they are working and you will become aware of talents and strengths you didn't know they had. If they believe you really see greatness in them, they will run farther, faster, harder, and happier for you (and the school and the kids) than they ever thought they could.

TRY THIS

- As a building leader, be a fan of your teachers' marathons. Believe in your teachers—even the ones you judge as lazy or lousy. Don't hate them for their flaws, love them for their gifts. Root for them.

- Be tireless in finding the majesty of their struggle. Never quit looking for their skills and talents—and use that to help them see it in themselves.

- Figure out together how you can help THEM achieve what they are doing. They're running the race, coach—not you.

DISCLAIMER

Some of your teachers and fellow administrators are slackers and jerks. It's true. There are folks who don't want to walk 10 feet for you or the kids, let alone run a marathon. It can be hard to root for lazy, manipulative people. But even those folks might change a little for a champion. Try hard to see what's great underneath all of that resistance. You have to believe there is a great runner in there. You might be surprised to find a real star who has been hidden for years. Your belief in their greatness is the greatest gift you can give them.

THE HOME TEAM

Do I not destroy my enemies when I make them my friends?
—Abraham Lincoln

Sure, he was my son. But I think to him they were all my sons. And I guess they were.
—Arthur Miller, *All My Sons*

My daughter Molly loves *The Ultimate Beastmaster*.
She's a superfan.

    The Ultimate Beastmaster is a Netflix program where contestants from different countries compete in an obstacle course called "The Beast." The fast-paced program is nominally about the competition but it's really about the contestants. Each show includes short background segments about the contestants, during which the audience learns more about them and their families. Often, the audience learns about obstacles of life that the contestants had to overcome to find themselves here at this obstacle course – where the contestants push themselves to the limit. And there, as they leap and hang and climb, you can lounge on your couch and find your body tighten as you will the contestants to move a little faster or hang on a little longer. You root for athletes that you have gotten to know.
    Unless you are Molly. Then, you root for Americans only and delight in the demise of all other contestants. Mexican and Brazil-

ian and Indian and Chinese and French athletes be damned.

When we are watching a movie and the characters aren't wearing uniforms to clearly indicate their allegiances, Molly always asks who are the good guys and who are the bad guys. She wants to know whose side she is on. If she's decided a character is a bad guy, then she doesn't mind when the dastardly character meets his dismal demise.

I should tell you: Molly is six years old. And as I write this, I am reflecting on what I've watched with her.

Dastardly Characters at Work

Like Molly, we work, often tacitly, to determine who is on our home team in our lives and at work. And after we figure that out, we root for them. And everyone else? Well, they can suffer and burn. In fact, that's kind of what we want. We delight in the failure of the "away team." It's natural— so natural that my six year old does it. But when your task is to lead, you end up working against yourself when you root against your people.

You can always find ways to see people as being on the "away" team. You don't like the way he talks in meetings. You hate the way she handles parents. Even the sound of his voice irritates you.

Reflect on this for a moment. Are you aware of the small ways in which you might actually be rooting against your own people? Think about the people at work— some of whom report directly to you— that you see as the "away" team. See their faces. What might happen if you saw those annoying jerks as part of your home team?

Consider this: study after study says that students perform better for teachers whom they believe love them. Also: workers try harder for bosses whom they believe genuinely care for them.

OTHERFUL PRINCIPLE

Treat all of your people as members of your home team—
even the ones who frustrate you.

QUICK SKIM

We are constantly determining who is on our home team. We treat
our home team well; we make allowances for them. When we determine that people are on the away team, we are more likely to treat
them badly and make assumptions about them. All people work
harder for people who are rooting for them.

TRY THIS

- Be aware of your tendency to root for some people and
  root against others. While this makes sense at a ballgame, it
  doesn't serve you very well as a leader to a broad group of
  diverse people.

- Ask yourself: what happens when the leader secretly roots
  against his/her own people?

- And then ask: what kind of strengths and tools would be
  more available to you if you saw all your teachers, administrators, staff, parents, and kids as your home team?

- Finally: which members of your team are being held back
  by you withholding your support? When you treat one of
  your people like they are on the away team, that's your fault
  not theirs.

DISCLAIMER

You might have some people at school who are actually working
against you. It's true that some people will budge for no man or

woman. But you don't have to wrestle with a pig. Remember that when you do, you get muddy and the pig has a great time. And, you never know, a hardened enemy from earlier in your career might become a valued comrade after years have gone by. You do yourself no favors by rooting against others, even when they behave like grade A jerks.

GETTING EVEN

Sometimes courage looks a lot like failure.
—Jessica Lahey, *The Gift of Failure*

Forgiveness says you are given another chance
to make a new beginning.
—Desmond Tutu

Words can sometimes, in moments of grace, attain
the quality of deeds.
—Elie Wiesel

Inevitably, the people who work for you at school will screw things up or screw you over.

They won't do what you tell them. They'll drop the ball on your watch and you'll have to eat the consequences. The test scores will be lower than you expected. Your teachers will tell you one thing and then do something else. Sometimes you'll work very hard on something, at great cost to yourself, and no one will care. You will stick your neck out for someone and they will not be grateful. You will be accused of intentions you did not have. There will be occasions when you will feel betrayed, disrespected, and unloved.

No leader in history can be spared this, by the way.

When you get cornswaggled at work, you will respond like a human being. You will feel lousy. You will be angry or frustrated and may want to get even. You may be tempted to have one of two powerful responses:

1. Get Aggressive. "I'm the BOSS! These people need to figure out what time it is. I have the power to humiliate/fire/transfer/destroy. They better do what they're supposed to do or I'm going to want heads on sticks!"

Whoa...

THIS IS STRESSFUL AND COUNTERPRODUCTIVE: It scares your people. It puts you and the teachers at odds and can raise the hackles of the union/teacher leaders. It can transform your school into a Gotcha Operation where people are watching their backs and rooting for others to make mistakes so they can remain under the radar.

2. Shut Down/CYA. "Screw this! I'm not ruining my career for people who don't respect how hard I work. I'm playing it safe, keeping my head down, and my door shut. This too shall pass."

DOING THIS DOESN'T WORK BECAUSE: Your people may stop trusting you. You diminish yourself and your responsibilities as the leader by deciding that when the going gets risky, you get lost. Worse, you teach all those people that work for you that there is no safety in their taking risks, either.

Both roads lead to the same place: a work environment with diminished creativity and less dynamic growth. Think about it. Nobody at school can learn from mistakes if no one wants to ever admit making them.

The way that school leaders handle errors—their own and those of others—gets hardwired into how the whole organization handles failure. As a leader, you're setting THE example when you lead—especially in a school. Whatever you do becomes "the way we do things around here."

The power move is what we call Productive Forgiveness. Show the people who work for you how to forgive and you show them how to take a punch. It takes a lot of strength to identify a small mistake as a small mistake. Sometimes letting something go can be the strongest move of all.

Still, you can't forgive everything. But as a leader at school, what you can't forgive should be a very short list—and correlate exactly with your district policies and state/federal law.

A Guide to Handling Mistakes at School: Productive Forgiveness

First, let's take a moment to look at the things that forgiveness is NOT:

Condoning: failing to see the action as wrong and in need of forgiveness

Excusing: not holding the offender as responsible for the action

Forgetting: removing awareness of the offense from consciousness

Forgiveness isn't about letting someone get away with a crime. Done properly, it can be a master stroke that transforms an error into a community builder.

1. Make a clear decision.
   Most mistakes will not be firing offenses—but you will need to decide quickly whether the offense falls into this category.
   - A big mistake might require legal or professional remedies—massive stuff. If someone needs to be canned or worse, consult the bargaining agreement and then handle it with expediency and care.
   - If it doesn't reach that threshold, put all your efforts towards fighting infection and swelling. Don't let a non-firing offense look like one. It'll create factions,

erode people's trust in you, and potentially become a referendum on your leadership.

2. Acknowledge the mistake to the offender and the offended.
    •   This can be done privately or publicly, depending on who is affected.
    •   Sharing this mistake with those who are not affected by the injury can destroy your reputation as a trustworthy leader, so proceed wisely.

3. Identify all the consequences to all parties.
    •   It can be good to encourage perps to identify all the potentially injured parties. Whatever their intent, they may have a spotty understanding of who they really hurt. Help them see the consequences of their actions.
    •   Use this as an opportunity for reconciliation for both the offender and the offended. Facilitate reflection on the part of the person who screwed up; allow for safe (but undeniably honest) grievance on the part of the victim. Bring them together in the same room if you can. And if you're the victim, model how to show disappointment without revenge.

4. Define and encourage reparations.
    •   Forgiveness cannot happen without statements and attempts to avoid repeated mistakes. Debts need to be made whole. As the leader, you can set the calendar and oversee that reparations are made as soon as possible.

5. Forgive and remember.
    •   The leader's job is to make sure that a skinned knee doesn't turn into gangrene. Your goal is to encourage scar tissue growth. It's amazing how a relatively minor mistake at school can turn into a massive problem

instead of a learning opportunity.

- If it doesn't end in jail time, the loss of credentials, or a sensationalized story on the news, let it go. Forgive, or you'll carry the poison with you. Remember so that you can monitor improvement, but resist the urge to keep score.

When we stop trying to get even, we free up room and energy to get better. And isn't that what school is all about?

●THERFUL PRINCIPLE

Productive Forgiveness promotes system-wide resilience and cultivates a positive culture of risk taking.

QUICK SKIM

When a situation (or a person) does you wrong at school, remember: you sometimes screw your people over, too. Don't be hobbled by anger and resentment. Vengeful leaders make terrible bosses. Graceful leaders use forgiveness as a power move. Use others' mistakes/crimes as an opportunity to make your organization more innovative and resilient. Model Productive Forgiveness and your whole school will get stronger.

Oh, and you'll need to forgive yourself sometimes, too.

TRY THIS

There's a long list above here, but to summarize Productive Forgiveness quickly:

- Talk to the offender and recognize the error as an error, in person/email/phone call. Be clear and as unemotional as you can muster. This can be private or public, depending on how many people were affected. It's a judgment call.

- Identify the consequences and all the people who are paying for them.

- Forgive and remember. Provide support. Share an example of an equal-sized mistake you have made. Use words like "humility," "compassion," and "awareness." Tell them things will go better next time. Tell them you are rooting for them and you'd like to hear from them. Tell them to remember how this feels. You remember, too.

DISCLAIMER

Wait... should you forgive everything?

Heck no.

If you need to fire or punish someone because of an error, do it cleanly and with dignity. Be clear and public about why. If you are constrained by a gag rule, then you must put your own reputation on the line as collateral. Schools are terrible places for secrets. If somebody gets punished and people don't know why, they will fill in the blanks with invented and often corrosive guesses. Some of the guesswork will be about you and your motives.

And that can hurt your most important currency: your reputation.

THE KID IS MORE IMPORTANT THAN THE CARPET

Because I love you, a bushel and a peck,
A bushel and a peck, though you make my heart a wreck.
You make my heart a wreck, and you make my life a mess,
Make my life a mess, yes, a mess of happiness,
About you. About you.

—Frank Loesser, "A Bushel and a Peck"

Clients do not come first. Employees come first.
If you take care of your employees, they will take care
of the clients.

—Richard Branson

My car used to be clean.

Don't get me wrong; I didn't wash it every day. But when I got into my car, there was nothing on the seats or in the pouches behind the seats or in the cupholders or in the slots in the door or on the floor in front of the seats or behind the back seats by the rear window or in between the seats. It was clean. I didn't take pride in it being clean. I didn't have to work at it. It just was.

Now, when I get into my car, there is stuff everywhere—stuff I have to apologize for as I shift it off of seats or from in front of seats, where people have politely tried to fit their legs, and out of cupholders, where they had rightfully expected to place their coffees.

And it's not just my car that's become a mess. I live with a wrecking crew of three little girls. They leave a wake of destruction wherever they go. And they never get tired. When I am cleaning one thing, they are destroying something else. Did I mention that they are also the sweetest little things you've ever seen? They melt my heart. And so I spend a lot of time cleaning things up.

But, I do get tired. And sometimes when I turn from what I've just cleaned to see something that newly requires cleaning, I get upset. And I yell. Like the time that I was sweeping the kitchen floor after dinner because my girls usually get more food on the floor than in their mouths. I was just about finished when one of my daughters spilled her milk on the living room carpet—yes, her milk. Oh, the irony. And I cried over it—well yelled, more like. Worried about the smell of sour milk that might haunt the carpet no matter how well I cleaned it, I launched into a forceful explanation to my delinquent children, letting them know that they were messing up. Messing everything up.

Then, my father stopped me and reminded me of something that I already knew, something so clear and obvious, and something that I'd forgotten again. He said, "The kid is more important than the carpet." And I looked at my frightened little girl, who had run to get paper towels to try to clean up the spill, and I wondered how I could get it all so wrong.

My father delights in my daughters. (So does my mother. Hey, Mom!) He doesn't allow his appreciation of them to be muddled by their being children and doing things that children do. When they say something funny or do something adorable, he catches my eye with a look that captures how lucky we are to be a part of these girls' lives. Grandparents get it because they have been through it all already. They lived it, and they know what's important. They know it's about the kids, not about them. They are more willing to meet children on their own terms.

The Grandparent Maneuver

As a leader, I try to approach things more like a grandparent than a parent. When my teachers have a bad day or make a mistake, I try to remember that they are more important than the momentary inconvenience of the mistake they made.

People make mistakes. People also make life worth living.

My daughters fill my life with joy. I can't even remember what the milk-defiled carpet looked like. And I don't care.

The teachers at your school are its most valuable asset. Yes, the children are what we all work for—but it's your teachers who serve the children and who, therefore, need your utmost concern. The children will come and go—just like the technology and the furniture and the supervisors. But your teachers will remain, the steadfast custodians of this thing we call "school." They'll be there long after you leave.

Don't let frustrating situations that you won't even remember in months or years to follow ruin your relationship with a teacher. And, for goodness sake, don't break their spirits because of your bad day, bad reaction, or limitations. The teachers take care of the students. It's your job to take care of the teachers.

OTHERFUL PRINCIPLE

Your most important job is to take care of your teachers.

QUICK SKIM

Our relationships with our people are more important than the frustration we might feel when things go awry. Be aware that your frustration with a teacher or colleague can cause you to confuse your priorities. Here's how the machinery of education works:

- Schools are made up of teachers. The students (and their parents) come and go.

- Teachers serve the students.

- Administrators serve the teachers.

As a leader, your people are your top priority. Always. Everything else—even that super pressing issue you have going on right now (the one that the board member or parent is asking about)—is relatively trivial. No amount of spilled milk should have the ability to rearrange your priorities.

TRY THIS

- Attend to your people and your interactions with them. Messy relationships are more destructive than messy situations. Let them know you care about them, over and over.

- When someone takes issue with something a teacher has done, direct that person to the teacher and let the teacher know that you are available to help.

- If a teacher comes to you with a mistake, focus first on helping the teacher work it out. You can always follow up later, if necessary, on how to avoid the mistake next time.

DISCLAIMER

You will need to be clear about things that aren't OK. Some of your people might spill the milk all the time and not even think that's a problem. Some of your people might be sensitive to you identifying the boundaries. If you've proven how important they really are to you, they'll take your rare critiques a lot better. And if they don't, honestly, there's only so much you can do. Don't get sucked into someone's thin-skinned, blackhole of bullsh*t.

YOU CAN DO THINGS NO ONE ELSE CAN

It is a good idea to obey all the rules when you're young
just so you'll have the strength to break them when you're old.

—Mark Twain

Render unto Caesar the things that are Caesar's,
and unto God the things that are God's.

—Matthew, 22:21

If I'd observed all the rules, I'd never have got anywhere.

—Marilyn Monroe

Few people outside of education get it.
It ain't like other gigs.
We need to be perfect.

Somewhere between the drive to be examples for the students and the requirement to serve our fiduciary responsibilities to taxpayers, we in education hold ourselves to, quite literally, the highest standards of integrity. Politicians, doctors, police officers, and the clergy get away with things we can't. Whether we're on vacation or at the grocery store, we know that people expect us to be good, decent, honest people who are always on the clock.

And because there are always just enough educators acting like real criminals out there to keep us in the news, we feel like we need to be way above reproach. We self-police like nobody's business. We know teachers and principals who won't even swear aloud, even when the students aren't around. And we understand why. We're supposed to be paragons of rule following, the last defense of what is civil and honorable. We are the Knights of the Realm.

You get this, right? It's absolutely bonkers, sure, but it's what so many of us believe, deep down in our school-loving hearts.

And so the idea of using your position in the hierarchy at school in order to bend—or circumvent—the rules might make you feel uncomfortable. And that's a very good thing.

But not all the time.

Why not always? Because leadership often demands action from us that the rule structure simply can't support. People—including teachers, kids, and their families—don't always fit perfectly into the boxes our states and school boards have made for them. To keep the ship afloat, to keep the trains running, and especially to address the dynamic needs of students, school leaders sometimes need to think outside the rule box.

And that's when you have to pull that altruistic power move of leadership: the power to break the rules.

Creative Insubordination

Let's be clear. There are some rules that should never be broken. Don't assault people, don't lie under oath, don't steal, don't change state test scores, and don't wear sweatpants to dinner. (Seriously, if you're not a child or a professional athlete, don't do that.)

We're talking about a particular power move of leadership, required since (and before) the days of Caesar crossing the Rubicon. My good friend Jim Lerman calls it "Creative Insubordination:" the power to work around the rules in order to do something good. We're talking about an advanced level of the game that every leader needs to learn to play. Inflexible insistence on the rules comes with a law of diminishing returns. All of the rules leave out some of the people. When we say things like "my hands are tied here" what we're sometimes saying to our people is that we aren't creative or committed enough to make something work.

The Real Power of Your Title

There are things that only you can do in your position at school. Whether it's in your classroom, the hallways, or the faculty meeting, your title gives you certain superpowers. Many of the most important things you will ever do for your people will be when you push the elasticity of the system to make room for something that really matters.

You can flip the power relationship at any time and put your people on top. For example, your people can't override you—unless you let them. Sometimes that's exactly what should happen. You can completely redefine what is "acceptable" for the people who work for you.

In fact, if you can't occasionally let someone get away with something, you'll never really get anyone's trust. Your teachers need to see that you understand that education is sometimes a rock fight—a battle in the streets where the biggest wins are when you can reduce the number of losers. A real warrior knows that the rules of the state aren't always the same as the rules of the street.

As a leader, you can use your place in the hierarchy to help your people. At the end of the day, it's the most meaningful power your title actually gives you.

For your people, you can...

Change the deadline.
Look the other way.
Throw blocks downfield.
Bend the rules.
Steal from Peter to pay Paul.

Distract the authorities.
Sign off on stuff.
Not write stuff down.
Keep your mouth shut.
Take the fall.
Let someone else be right.

And most of all, the very best thing you can do is to get the hell out of their way.

OTHERFUL PRINCIPLE

Sometimes thinking around the rules
is the best way to serve your school.

QUICK SKIM

People in education don't ever want to break the rules. That's a great thing—except when it isn't. The rules don't always work—and in school, it's not one size fits all. As a leader at school, sometimes that means you have to color outside the lines. Use your power in the hierarchy to help your people. Your teachers, colleagues, and kids need you to have their backs—even if that means you have to wave away the power of an expectation, rule, or guideline. You have to be open to the possibility that the rules should serve the growth of your people, not the other way around.

TRY THIS

Identify any rules or expectations that seem to be counterproductive. Think about teachers or colleagues who are hobbled by guidelines that don't need to be so stringent. Start easy. Letting somebody off the hook for something might be just the thing that allows them to trust you. Remember: you didn't get into this gig to enforce rules. You came here to improve lives.

DISCLAIMER

For goodness sake, don't break a rule that will hurt a student, burn your people, or endanger your credentials. Also: don't ever give away your integrity. It's really hard to get back.

PART 3

CONTEXTING

Contexting
is communicating with the
understanding that what others hear
is more important than what you say.

As a leader, you must pay attention to how other people under-stand things. When you think like a Contexter, you study how others communicate. You come to learn how other people describe and experience things.

You learn how other people learn. This is how you gain influ-ence.

Leaders cannot choose their followers. Their followers choose them.

Leaders who understand this become more attuned to what other people care about and how they think. They speak in the language of the listener.

When you think like a Contexter, you realize that there is no such thing as "teaching." There is only assisted learning. Likewise, there is no such thing as "leadership." There is only assisted growth.

When those you try to lead understand what you are trying to do in their own words and frames, they will do the work you want them to do, for themselves.

MACH'S PRINCIPLE: AN INTRODUCTION TO CONTEXTING

In nature we never see anything isolated
but everything in connection with something else,
which is before it, beside it, under it and over it.

—Johann Wolfgang von Goethe

Everything is everything...
All we need is dedication
Let me tell ya that

—Lauryn Hill

I never explain anything.

—Mary Poppins

Isaac Newton believed a lot could be learned from a bucket filled with water.

Of course, Newton believed something could be learned from anything. A piece of glass in sunlight taught him about light frequencies. Marbles taught him about thermodynamics. An apple taught him about gravity.

Newton's experiments grew out of his curiosity about the world around him and his inkling that there might be more going on than meets the eye. His willingness to try new things helped him invent calculus and physics, which you shouldn't hold against him, no matter how you felt about those classes in high school.

And while we all know the name Isaac Newton, many of us have never heard of how one of his experiments inspired a scientist named Ernst Mach (of Mach Speed fame) to explore the interconnectedness of things. In turn, the lesser known Mach, who lived a couple of centuries after Newton, ended up creating the context to enable a certain office clerk in Switzerland to uncover the most famous scientific formula in the world.

Albert Einstein's Theory of Special Relativity changed the course of scientific exploration. And while you might have no idea what E=mc2 means, you might be tickled by how its sister, the Theory of General Relativity, relates to the work of leadership. For now, all you have to do is enjoy a story about three scientists and two experiments– and how the context they gave each other might help you become a better communicator.

Newton and his Bucket Experiment

Newton imagined that there might be relationships in the cosmos that most people didn't see. His "Bucket Experiment" was his exploration of how human understanding is limited when isolated from outside experience. The experiment is so simple you could do it at home yourself.

Find a bucket with a handle. Attach a rope to the middle of the handle and fill the bucket with water. Now, hold the rope in one hand and rotate the bucket with the other hand, and watch what the water does. As the bucket spins, the water slowly begins to spin, too. The water near the edges moves more and more rapidly, slowly beginning to creep up the walls of the bucket while the water in the middle moves more slowly. It's good to do this alone and not drunk, if possible.

Newton recognized that the water moved because the bucket

moved. While his observation takes little imagination, his further thoughts about it do. Pretend you live inside the bucket, can't see outside of it, and have no reference but the bucket (let's imagine that the bucket is your whole world, kind of like how some American football fans act during Super Bowl week). You would have no understanding of why the water started to climb up the walls of the bucket any more than you can "feel" the world spinning under your feet right now. Without a relative point outside the bucket, your guesses as to what was happening would be incredibly limited. Think of it this way: if the sun didn't "travel" across the sky, what proof would you have that the earth is spinning?

This notion of connected phenomena delighted and intrigued Newton, but he did little with it aside from talk about motion and inertia. Ernst Mach, a couple of centuries later, used Newton's experiment as the context to do an even crazier experiment. One you can, again, do yourself. And you don't even need a bucket.

Mach and his Star Experiment

Go out on a clear night, somewhere you can actually see the stars. Look straight up into the sky and start to spin around, as if you were a bucket in the 17th century. Notice three things: the stars appear to be "circling around you" with the ones over top your head going slower than the stars closer to the horizon. Also notice that your arms begin to pull away from your body the faster you spin (recall: "centrifugal force"). Finally, notice that you are alone, spinning around and looking up into the sky in the middle of the night. All this leadership work is starting to make you do pretty weird things. Just sayin'.

Mach theorized that your arms floating upward were directly related to the stars spinning– that if you saw stars spinning, then your body would simultaneously have to be experiencing centrifugal force. Mach wondered: do stars that are millions of miles away therefore have a relationship with the movement of our bodies? His guess: yes, they do.

Einstein and his Theory of Almost Everything

Einstein was intrigued with Mach's insight and dubbed it "Mach's Principle," using it as an essential context for his work on General Relativity. Inspired by Mach, Einstein would write, "a particle's inertia is due to some interaction of that particle with all the other masses in the universe." While Einstein would later abandon Mach's Principle (the math didn't really hold up), his work would monumentally move the conversation forward in science's attempt to find the connections between all things. Today, debates about things such as string theory, entanglement, and the Higgs-Boson particle continue to reflect our often not-simply-scientific desire to find a Theory of Everything.

Newton had his bucket. Mach had his arms and stars. Einstein had his mathematics. Great scientists are always looking for the frame that reveals the relationships between things.

You might be, too.

You might be a fan of the Butterfly Effect, in which a butterfly flapping its wings in Beijing causes a tornado in Wichita. You might be a Moneyball gambler who sees every piece of meaningless-looking data as a yet-to-be-understood number that could help you draft your next Fantasy Football team. Maybe you are a data scientist who trusts that any behavior can be explained if you just look hard enough for the yet-to-be-known data that proves it. Or maybe you're someone who's just starting to consider interconnectedness for the first time.

Our theory?

If you are willing to put in the time to really learn about other people's expertise and knowledge, you can use this understanding to become an extraordinarily powerful communicator. When you know how to use the context of other people's worlds to help them understand things on their own terms, you can get people to understand nearly anything. And if you believe that everything can be connected, then finding the right context becomes inevitable.

The key is to listen and speak in the codes, stories, and shapes of others' expertise.

They (Not You) Connect the Dots

People don't learn something simply because they are taught it. People only understand something new when they connect it to something that is already important to them. Educators call this "Prior Knowledge." It's why great teachers spend a lot of energy learning what students already know about. Each person's prior knowledge is a guide, a not-yet-completed map with roads leading to new ideas.

Humans are hardwired to be delighted by making connections and their own sense of something. When a person suddenly "gets" something complicated or otherwise unknown, the hardest, most sought after thing becomes possible: people can change.

It's not about what YOU say. It's about what THEY hear. The connections must belong to them, not you. No matter how much something makes sense to you, other people must make those essential connections themselves.

So don't waste much time trying to explain things to people. It doesn't really work.

Instead, create context out of what your listeners already know. Custom build the frame for people to learn for themselves what you want to share. The best move is to let go of trying to control how other people connect to things. Your task is to keep trying landscapes that allow for them to find their own connections. Give them context and let them discover. When you acknowledge this and begin to work from it, you will tectonically shift how you construct relationships with your teachers, colleagues, parents, and students.

This is the great work of teaching and leading, for they are one in the same. When you study the great thought leaders (which is simply another word for teachers) in the history of the world, you find that they aren't explainers, they aren't coercers, they aren't even leaders.

They are "Contexters."

OTHERFUL PRINCIPLE

What you say is less important than what they hear.

QUICK SKIM

Leaders should stop explaining things.

"Explaining" puts the Explainer at the center of the world instead of who should be at the center: the Learner. This is as true in the classroom as it is in the faculty meeting.

Instead, be a "Contexter." Speak to your people in metaphors and ideas that they already know in order to give your listeners personal context. You must trust that those you lead can figure out nearly anything if the right context is provided to them. When you know how to use the context of people's worlds to help them understand things on their own terms, you can get people to understand nearly anything. Never forget that the only way people truly own an understanding is if they understand it in a way that is relevant to their own life.

TRY THIS

- Don't tell people what you think they should know. Help others understand things for themselves.

- Find out how people hear things. Pay attention to what works for them, their own areas of comfort and expertise. Whatever people already know can be used to help them begin to think about what they don't know.

- And if they don't get it, try another context, then another. If you're relentless, you'll find a way for them to understand it for themselves.

- Need a model for how to explain without explaining?

  1. OFFER THE FRAME

      The frame is a metaphor, an analogy, or a place of common ground. You cannot explain a damn thing. Don't forget this. You can, however, find the frame that allows someone else to figure out what you are trying to communicate. The more bespoke the frame, the more familiar or comfortable the frame for your audience, the more they will own the idea you are communicating.

  2. TRANSFER POWER

      Once you find a frame that works for your audience, hand it off. Give them chances to play with the idea they now own. They will become more invested the more they understand it. When people truly believe something is about them, they can own it and do something with it.

DISCLAIMER

There is no shortcut to creating good metaphors and frames for your people. Not all frames work for all people– and this can be terribly frustrating. Contexting is not about tricking or schmoozing people to agree with you. Cutting corners on this will make people think you are out of touch at best, manipulative at worst.

A football metaphor might be good for many Phys Ed teachers– but something having to do with nutrition or sportsmanship might work better for others. You can't simply drop a story about Magellan to connect with all history teachers any more than you can use your Shel Silverstein anecdote to connect with all third grade teachers.

If you don't put the time in to continually try to communicate in new contexts and frames, then you will fail. There are no vending machines of learning in this business—or in any other business, either.

STRANGER IN A STRANGE LAND

Personally I am very fond of strawberries and cream, but I have found that for some strange reason, fish prefer worms. So when I went fishing, I didn't think about what I wanted. I thought about what they wanted. I didn't bait the hook with strawberries and cream. Rather, I dangled a worm or grasshopper in front of the fish and said: 'Wouldn't you like to have that?' Why not use the same common sense when fishing for people?

—Dale Carnegie

I eat with people, and what has happened over the years because of that simple willingness to sit down and eat with people is that they have told me extraordinary things. They open up their lives to me in ways that I hadn't anticipated.

—Anthony Bourdain

Definitions belong to the definers, not the defined.

—Toni Morrison

I was a picky eater when I was kid.

Butter noodles, pizza, hamburgers, hoagies, and fries were my jam. Sometimes I spiced it up with deep fried fish or turkey loaf (please don't look that up if you don't know what it is). Green beans and carrots were the only vegetables that got through my defenses—the rest of it was definitely not for me.

I grew up in a white suburb outside of Philadelphia, a very small world of culinary choices. I liked what I liked and hated everything else. And I took my narrow-minded mindset right off to university, avoiding anything weird at the cafeteria. I'd go out with friends and stick to my guns. "No, I don't want to try the sushi, thank you very much."

That is until I went to Kenya and Tanzania in my last semester of college. As part of a University service trip, I and a small group of students flew to Nairobi to observe and work in a few schools and hospitals on the edge of the Serengeti. Our team, all studying to be teachers, nurses, or doctors, had to dig deep to get there. We'd fund-raised, held car washes and raffles, and worked extra hours outside of school. We begged our families for loans. To prepare, we took lessons in Kiswahili, studied the culture of the Maasai, and watched any movie that had anything to do with Africa. We'd planned to learn everything we could, help however possible, and let the cultures of these nations impact us—all of which we ended up doing.

It was a trip of a lifetime. And I, of course, began it like a champion moron.

After our long trip to Nairobi, we were taken to a nearby school and seminary where we'd be staying. The teachers, priests, and workers there welcomed us with smiles, music, and a huge feast. And within those first three hours of landing in Kenya, I managed to insult our hosts, shame our leaders, and make a horse's ass of myself. How, you ask? With my reaction to the food at our first meal.

I hadn't really prepared myself for what it was going to be like to be an honored guest at a table with food I'd never seen before. And that's probably why, when they passed the bowl of rice and meat around, I decided to ham it up to cover up how nervous I was to try any of it. I was a wise-cracking idiot, joking about the "Ebola stew" that was put in front of me. "Hey can somebody pass me the dengue fever sauce?" My friends laughed and I laughed as I scooped a little rice on my plate, carefully avoiding any of the strange looking meat or vegetables. The school leader of my trip, a missionary Catholic priest named Father Don, pulled me out of the hall, practically by the ear, and put me in my place.

"You are embarrassing me, our hosts, and yourself. These people are proud of who they are and the food they put on the table. They slaughtered a goat in our honor and are feeding us vegetables they have tended and harvested. You look and sound like a child. You are a guest here! It is YOUR job to meet these people where THEY are, not the other way around."

My face turned purple. I felt like a complete jerk. I was taking everyone for granted, self-absorbed and ignorant. I was ashamed of myself. But before I could go any further down the hole of disappointment, Father Don stopped me.

"I know you feel stupid—and you've behaved terribly. But you can fix this. Look at it this way: generosity isn't just about giving. It's also about receiving. Being a humble and willing guest is a priceless gift."

Father Don had gotten me right between the eyes and, thank goodness, I was ready to hear it. It did the trick: not only did I knock off the bad comedy, I started to eat everything. I ate it all: antelope, ugali, goat— and I suddenly transformed from a tourist to a traveler. I was no longer eating— I was discovering.

In East Africa, I gained a powerful insight about teaching and leadership. When in someone else's world, seeing their world the way they see it is much more important than seeing it the way I see it. As much as I could handle, I had to let go of my own boundaries, preferences, and methods. Acting as a humble visitor, I could make room for the "world of the other" to fill me. I could experience new things more fully.

My curiosity came alive. In short: I had to give myself over to being a learner. Thousands of miles from home, I had to accept that I was not the center of the universe. It's a powerful lesson that I've come to find many leaders must learn over and over again.

Great Leaders Are Contexters

There are a handful of truths that you can never forget when you are in charge at school.

- You cannot change anyone.

- You cannot make anyone do anything.

- You cannot even teach anyone anything, really.

What can you do? Help others to change themselves. Your people don't need someone to fix them; they need someone to understand them. To be a great leader, paradoxically, you should avoid leading as much as you can. Instead, pay attention. Listen. Learn from those you serve—they are the real masters. Only after an authentic effort to understand and appreciate your teachers can you begin to do anything to help them. It's about using your listener's context to communicate.

As a Contexter, you have two jobs:

1. To understand how others make meaning of things

2. To speak to others in their language and their context, not yours

Nothing and no one can be truly known without appreciating or being aware of context. Contexters make it their business to understand and describe, rather than control and prescribe.

Be Their Guest

So it is with your teachers, colleagues, students, and everyone else. Your mission must be to see other people's worlds as more important to them than anything you might introduce. As we mention in another essay, people are driven by our own fears, interests, responsibilities, and experiences (FIRE)—and these will always dwarf your wishes for them. No matter how much you try to make your beliefs more important to them than their own, you will fail.

Anything you introduce—any idea, prescription, suggestion—must be delivered to them in their language, in their custom, and according to their already formed worldview. People will not even hear you if you do not speak in a way that makes sense to them.

To do this, you must never stop trying to see and understand as others do. You are a visitor in the worlds of your teachers; it will never be your country. When you try to get the teachers to speak your language—rather than you trying to speak theirs—you limit your ability to coach them and bridle your ability to even see what they are doing.

Only after you understand that you are the foreigner can you begin to co-create conditions, inspire ways of thinking, and set the direction of where to go. Your goal should be influence, not control.

Then, you can join in THEIR efforts to be successful.

OTHERFUL PRINCIPLE

Great leaders don't try to change anyone.
They know they can only help others change themselves.

QUICK SKIM

Curriculum, instruction, and tests belong to the teachers. They are the ones tasked with administering this work. School leaders who do not teach will always be foreigners in this space. You must attempt to lead them as little as you can. Instead, learn from them. Find out what they believe and how they work. Use their words and expressions when you speak with them. Give yourself over to their ownership so you can free yourself to serve them. Work to help them improve their practice, instead of directing them, and you will make the brilliant trade of control for influence.

TRY THIS

- When you call them "my teachers," flip the ownership. Rather than MY teachers, think my TEACHERS. You learn from them; you don't own them.

- "Bad teaching" (like bad leadership) doesn't just happen. People have reasons for everything they do. Be relentless in trying to understand your teachers instead of judging, labeling, or (yikes) joking about them. Even the worst practices began as a rational thought.

- Visit classes more frequently—not to evaluate practice but to learn about your teachers and to spend time with them. Be a humble student in their class, not a judge of their world. Take notes as infrequently as you can.

- Remember, with most teachers you have to earn your visa. This happens when you honor their systems and use their words. Describe, don't prescribe.

DISCLAIMER

Sometimes, the local customs will be disturbing to you. You will want to jump in and stop things. Take pause. You might, indeed, need to oust the local chief. If so, do it quickly and as cleanly as possible. But unless you are prepared and able to do the heavy work to depose the leader and start nation building, you should evaluate your diplomatic options. It'll probably begin with eating food you think you don't like.

WHAT I LEARNED AT WINE CAMP

In order to influence someone, you need to know what already influences them… you must make a commitment to listening deeply so you can truly connect with and get through to [them].

—Tony Robbins

No law or ordinance is mightier than comprehending someone.

—Plato

…if we have to learn with each other we should also learn about each other so we can bring each other up.

—Chris Emdin

Aubrey walked us through towering, blonde oak shelves of bottles.

His store, tucked into the high end junk shops at Fisherman's Wharf in San Francisco, felt more like an old library than a wine shop. He'd carefully divided the store into boroughs of geographic provenance and then by neighborhoods of grape varietal and vintage. Small, handwritten placards were tacked on every shelf with details about mouth feel and flavor.

As Aubrey led me and a friend through the wine maze he'd built in this tourist trap, he told us stories about the wines as if they were old lovers. "I don't drink that one anymore but I definitely recommend. She'll break you at night but leave you happy in the morning." Aubrey killed me. His jokes were funnier because of his British accent. He wore an ascot.

I was new to wine at the time, a pretender who was looking for a sophisticated and cost effective way to look cool. I wanted to sit in an expensive restaurant like a badass, casually making my way around an impressive wine list. I aspired to bring a rare vintage to a dinner party and impress everyone with my erudite and supercool bottle choice.

The year before, I and a few other teachers at my school had somehow gotten approval from my school to take a wine class at Temple University as professional development. In most states, new teachers have to get a certain number of credits to earn permanent certification; naturally, I'd rather study booze than "differentiated instruction."

Every week we would focus on a different grape by studying six different wines, which meant we got to drink the entire 90 minute class. We cozied up to the professor for more generous pours during the lesson. It was basically an excuse to get buzzed in a classroom on a Friday night, a particular delight to me at the beginning of my teaching career.

I confess: I didn't learn much at wine camp.

But I did gain a respect for how broad and deep the world of wine is. It wasn't just about flavors or food pairing. There was the unique history of each vineyard. There were variations in vintner methods across the world, with stories of geniuses and renegades who created everything from champagne to white zinfandel.

So when Aubrey held forth about "terroir," standing like the Minotaur at the center of his wine labyrinth, I was in the right state of mind to hear it. "Americans talk about grape varieties. Everything is 'chardonnay,' 'cabernet sauvignon,' or 'merlot.' And that's fine. But in the Old World, we talk about the grapes AND the wine regions, like 'Montepulciano,' 'Bordeaux,' or 'Douro.'"

He looked at his bottles affectionately. "You must know where the wine is grown!"

Terroir

Terroir is a French word pronounced "terr-WAR." It comes from the latin root for "land." Studying a wine's terroir gives you insight on the conditions that made the wine possible. You look for the taste of the blazing Spanish sun in your tempranillo or the Loire Valley's chalky soil in your champagne. You aren't just drinking a glass of wine; you're drinking the land and the culture that produced it.

And that's the point: learning a wine's terroir doesn't just give you more information about the wine. It enriches how you experience the wine. You get a broader, deeper understanding of it.

Aubrey smartly upsold me on a Charter Oak Zinfandel for $45. At the time it was a fortune to me, the most expensive bottle of wine I'd ever bought. But I was happy to part with my money because I took home more than a bottle of wine. I took home a story: the who, where, and when of a complex and slowly developed grape juice.

Everyone Has Terroir

As an administrator, you are in the business of human development.

Every teacher who works for you has a social identity and a rich history. They come from somewhere with specific tales of families and friends; of wins and losses; and of moments of profound beauty and sadness. The lifetime of experiences that brought this person to your school has defined that person.

If you want to do the work of great leadership in schools, you have to start with your teachers' and colleagues' stories. Learn who they are. Learn about their families and where they came from. Listen to their anecdotes about growing up or their college days—and remember them. Are they married, do they have kids and/or a close group of friends? Who are those people? Pay attention to what they care about, especially what about teaching turns them on and off. The teachers who report to you are complex individuals.

You cannot lead them until you understand them.

Take a moment right now to think about the educators who work with and for you.

What do you know about their stories? What do you know about their terroir? When you care about other people's backgrounds and stories, you'll begin to apprehend their complexity and beauty. They'll become more human to you. These teachers, and their skills and abilities, are the most valuable asset in your school system. Respect how fundamental and vital it is that you truly know and appreciate what these teachers are bringing to their classrooms.

Think again about wine. Without any knowledge of terroir, we are limited to making decisions about wines based on their color, price, or someone else's evaluation. Many of us have ordered a bottle based on such thinking. And when we get the cheap stuff, we often remark how we can't tell the difference.

Is that how you want to be about your people and their talents?

●THERFUL PRINCIPLE

Learn about, respect, and cherish where your people come from.

●UICK SKIM

People are like wine. You have to know their regions, stories, and vintages if you want to understand and develop their potential and quality. That's your job. Your expertise should be about understanding who your people are. In fields like education, you simply can't separate a person's work from the person. How they teach is an expression of who they are as a human being. The best way to truly develop and influence your teachers is to put in the time and dig deep into knowing them as well as you can.

TRY THIS

- Learn as much as you can about the people who work at your school. Find out about their families, their personal lives, and the way they like to think and grow. Be honored that they share it with you.

- Jump in and take over when they have a daytime emergency —recognize and model that family is always first. Nothing says "I care about you and your world" more.

- Be careful. We work in schools that, at scale, threaten to reduce all behavior to data points. Teachers are best known (and supported) by those who appreciate their backgrounds and choices, not by their observation reports or students' test scores. Seeing that a wine has received a "93/100" from the Wine Spectator might give you a sense of that wine— but it does not replace sipping it with an understanding of its terroir.

DISCLAIMER

Sometimes you have to deny tenure or let someone go because they are hurting the organization or taking up valuable space. That's part of the job. The more you know about your people, the better you can let a low performer go with a clear head (you did everything you could) and the ability to offer targeted support for their next move.

When you do sack someone, remember that the other teachers will need added assurance that you know their terroir as well and that they are safe to keep on growing. But tread carefully: being known as that boss who "kills the weak" can also encourage your rising stars to play CYA all day. And that's how you turn your school system into a beauty pageant where everyone only shows the good whenever you are around—and hides everything else they can from you.

FACULTY MEETING
OF BABEL

We're all islands shouting lies to each other across seas
of misunderstanding.

—Rudyard Kipling, *The Light That Failed*

We never listen when we are eager to speak.

—Francois de la Rochefoucauld

I'm just a soul whose intentions are good
Oh Lord, please don't let me be misunderstood

—Nina Simone

I've always admired (and been secretly jealous of) people who are
multilingual.

I can swing a few phrases in Spanish and French—order a
beer, say "I'm sorry," find out where they sell the good cheese: you
know, essential travel stuff. But I'm pretty useless when it comes
to engaging in meaningful conversations in anything but my native
tongue.

A couple of years ago, my wife and I flew from New York
City to Sydney, Australia to visit a friend and had a short layover
in Guangzhou, China. The smartly dressed flight attendants on
China Southern, a terrific airline I'd never heard of before this trip,
casually switched back and forth from Chinese to English. I felt like

a complete moron, trapped in my mono-linguism.

I hate to admit it, but I'd never even heard of Guangzhou. My friend Maram reminded me that it was a major port city on the Silk Road. "You must have learned about this in high school," she said, eyes wide open. I have no memory if I did. Here's what I know now: this town I'd never heard of is bigger than New York City. In fact, its population is bigger than NYC, Philly, Boston, and Chicago combined.

How did I have a blindspot that big?

I was awed by Guangzhou and the people who live there. It's an amazing place with ancient city walls slowly decaying in the shadows of soaring skyscrapers. People riding bikes, driving Mercedes, and pulling rickshaws all share the same roads. The food was brilliant and wild: fiery soups filled with peanuts, noodles, and cilantro served with dumplings filled with meat. My wife and I could not name a single item on the menu and just kind of pointed to things. We had to act out things for people around us to get directions and help.

But mostly, I was anxious and a little paralyzed. Walking down the street, I suddenly forgot the few Chinese expressions I had learned for fear that I'd mispronounce something. I was overtaken by a deep desire to be whisked away to LA or London, somewhere I felt I'd be understood without an effort that I was helpless to mount.

When we fear being misunderstood, we can feel lost and powerless. Even our personalities can change as we become a sliver of ourselves, worried to offend or be judged for not knowing how to behave.

Everyone Speaks a Different Language

So much of people exists in the way they speak— their words, expressions, body language, facial expressions. In the act of explaining an idea or expressing ourselves, we are at our most personal and honest. Shared understanding is intimate and allows for deeper, more sophisticated connections. It enables a warmth and encourages cooperation. All human relationships are built on how we communicate with each other.

We often assume that we all speak the same language, especially when we speak in the same language. This assumption is one of the most insidious dangers in all of leadership.

The truth is much closer to the idea that everyone speaks his or her own language, in a way. Each of us has our own bespoke tongue: complete with a unique syntax, idioms, inflections, and even vocabulary that requires someone else's translation.

There is only a small group of people who actually understand you most of the time. Maybe it's a sibling or an old friend. They "get" you, almost reading your mind when you are about to say something. Occasionally, they can even finish your sentences. Then there are those who almost always misunderstand you. They are confused and need you to explain it a different way. They are some-times insulted by things that you say—and you have no idea why.

The fact is: we do not speak each other's languages very well. Accepting that—and the resulting responsibility that follows—is a critical foundation of your work as a leader.

It's a Mess, Just As It Should Be

All the people who work at your school are trapped in their brains and ways of communicating. As are you. Even the most self-actualized people in your building or department have trouble seeing their own ways of thinking while they are thinking. A lot of misunderstanding grows out of people not really understanding how other people think.

We have to expect people to be confused by us. It's inevitable and unstoppable. All the awkwardness and discomfort is the price of doing any communication business. We must make room for (and our peace with) it, patiently and tirelessly working to untangle knots.

Don't let misunderstanding become a toxin. Beware of how dangerous it can be. The worst rifts at work come when a misun-derstanding somehow becomes a referendum on the health of the system. Misunderstandings slow things down, yes. They are a pain in the neck. But they will happen, and a good leader helps the team learn and grow from misunderstandings.

Your task is to be a diplomat, constantly in search of ways to meet other people where they are and how they think. Leaders who can help others become comfortable with the many languages that exist in an organization can have tremendous impact on morale.

The power isn't in helping others being understood.

It's in helping others understand and respect how other people understand. Yes, definitely read that again.

Decriminalize confusion for your people and they'll get more done, spend less time at each others' throats, and maybe even spend more time laughing good heartedly at how hard it is to understand anything anybody is trying to say.

●THERFUL PRINCIPLE

Expect confusion. Avoid being irritated by this—
it will only distract you and lower morale.

QUICK SKIM

- People misunderstand each other all the time. It's the human condition—not a flaw to be stamped out.

- Most problems in any organization are miscommunication problems.

- As a leader, model how to work hard at understanding others. Learn to speak their language. Be an enthusiastic student of how others talk and listen.

- "One size fits all" is a terrible rule for schools—and especially for teachers. Each educator at your school is different. Most of your interactions with them should be custom made for each of them, informed by the efforts you put in to understand them.

TRY THIS

Take the sting out of misunderstanding with any of these classic, great leader moves:

- Acknowledge that confusion isn't a crime. It isn't proof that someone is evil, lazy, or crazy. It's a part of all communication.

- Kindly laugh at yourself when you misspeak or misunderstand. Show your people how to do it. Admit when you've made a mess of an explanation but without shame, defensiveness, or self-deprecation.

- Bless the wide variety of teaching styles at your school. Talk it up, be proud of it.

- Publicly admire when someone restates something better than you did.

- Ask for feedback at the meeting ("Does this make sense?" "Is there a better way I could put this?").

- Ask for clarification in a warm way ("Would you mind explaining that a different way? I'm sure it's me—I just don't quite get it").

- Smile when you're asked the same question. And then explain it again in a different way. And then again.

DISCLAIMER

Some miscommunication can be incredibly dangerous. Areas of your job, such as building security, student and teacher well-being, and fulfilling state mandates need as much middle-of-the-day clarity as you can muster. This is not an essay promoting being sloppy. Just don't cry wolf when it's really a puppy. In fact, when you let benign misunderstandings be benign, then you'll actually increase the chance that you can quickly clear up dangerous miscommunications. If you demand to be clear about everything, sometimes you'll end up being unclear about something very important.

LET ME TELL YOU

So long as men can breathe or eyes can see
So long lives this, and this gives life to thee.
—William Shakespeare, Sonnet 18

and if you don't know, now you know
—Notorious B.I.G.

I hadn't realized how handsome Alexander Hamilton was until I saw the redesign of the $10 bill in 2000.

When the new bill was first issued, old and newly designed bills circulated together. I remember comparing them on a line at Taco Bell and thinking that if Hamilton could see the redesign, he'd be pleased. I thought, then, that this was the biggest facelift this founding father was likely to get.

15 years later, I was walking with my wife to see *Les Miserables* on Broadway. We'd both seen the show before, but we loved the music and wanted to see the new production. It was great. But getting there was more of a hassle than usual—which is something to say for Times Square. I made the mistake of turning down 46th street and walking into what I later learned was the opening night of *Hamilton* on Broadway. It was a scene.

Earlier that summer, Jack Lew, the 76th Secretary of the Treasury, announced that Alexander Hamilton, the 1st Secretary of the Treasury, would be forfeiting his spot on the front of the $10 bill to make room for a deserving, yet-to-be-named woman. We could expect the new $10 bill in 2020.

That Hamilton was targeted as the face to be shifted off the front of a bill is not surprising, not when you consider the other faces on the bills: Washington, Lincoln—they were big-time presidents. Jackson, Old Hickory—he was a president, too. Grant? He was a general and a president. And Franklin wasn't a president, but he did something with a key and a kite, right? So, there was Hamilton. What did he do again? He wasn't a president, was he?

Then, *Hamilton* was nominated for 16 Tony Awards and won a Grammy for best musical theater album and the Pulitzer Prize for Drama. Now, everyone was talking about *Hamilton*—the musical and the man. What did he do? A ton, which now even my daughters could tell you about. The treasury department dropped dropping Hamilton.

If You See Something (Great), Say Something

Everyone is busy at school. It's easy to mistake what's urgent for what's important.

There are teachers

- writing college recommendations for students during their lunch periods
- lending money to a kid and never expecting it back
- sharing a personal story of loss to console a student in grief
- scouring the internet for contests and scholarships for kids who need a shot
- starting a robotics club and then hustling to learn more about robots
- hanging back in the art studio after school for a kid who wants to practice
- bringing in remnants from rugs that used to adorn their own living rooms
- inventing creative and commensurate ways for a kid to

complete a project
- handwriting a note of encouragement for a lonely student
- inviting a student to try out for the team or play
- planning their summers and family vacations around lesson plans they're building

There is likely a teacher doing one of these things right now, even as you read this. And there are tons of other great things happening in classrooms every day.

Who's going to shed light on and magnify these and other easy-to-overlook moments?

The answer, my friend, is YOU.

As a leader, you have a platform to tell parents how great your teachers are. Your school board, too, needs examples of how your school is actually doing miracles every day. And your teachers and fellow admin need to hear it, as well. It's not simply that teachers need validation. Some of them don't even see how great they are—and that's actually stunting their growth.

Stories shape our world. A well told story has the power to change how we see things we used to not see and make us care about things we didn't care about before. The stories we tell and how we tell them can change the way students, parents, and other leaders see the teachers—even how the teachers see themselves.

The stories we tell ourselves about our teachers might change the way we see them, too.

●THERFUL PRINCIPLE

The stories you tell about your people can change the way
your people are seen and appreciated.

QUICK SKIM

Our platform to tell our teachers' stories is a powerful asset. Use it. The stories we tell about our teachers and how we tell those stories impacts how everyone sees them and their work. We can change the culture of a school through the stories we tell.

TRY THIS

- Make time in your schedule for the sole focus of seeing teachers' greatness. Share specific stories of what you saw with administrators, teachers, or parents who weren't there.

- Don't let other urgent calls for your attention cause you to deprioritize or skip this. It isn't gravy. People are telling stories about your school. Their stories might be about what's not going well. Are you going to let those narratives win?

- Take on the role of storyteller: Sculpt the stories. Highlight the easily missed details. Identify the heroics of your team members.

DISCLAIMER

Don't lie. Don't cover for crime or negligence. Recognize that a very small percentage of your teachers and fellow admin are actually doing terrible work. And when you see that, address it with candor, speed, and the required actions. Just make sure to highlight the good stuff happening around the bad stuff.

And if you're not working to fire someone, then you better have a few good stories to tell about them.

THE MAGIC FEATHER

If we treat people as if they were what they could be,
we help them become
what they are capable of becoming.

—Johann Wolfgang von Goethe

Teaching is hard work, and to do it well,
staff have to not just work hard,
but work inspired.

—Amy Fast, Ed.D.

We few, we happy few, we band of brothers;
For he to-day that sheds his blood with me
Shall be my brother

—William Shakespeare, *Henry V*

The voice on the other end of the line waited for me to respond.

I was thinking it over, playing out in a speeding blur the many
things I'd have to do to say "yes." The people I'd have to leave, the
packing I'd have to do, the resignation letter I'd have to write to
the school board. I thought of moving away from my family and
friends. I'd never really considered what it would mean to leave my
home state of Pennsylvania.

But, to be honest, one thing dominated my thoughts as I considered taking a new teaching job at a competitive, high-powered,

affluent, and intimidatingly-accomplished school district on Long Island. All I could really think about was whether or not I was good enough at teaching. And, in my heart, I was pretty sure that I wasn't.

After four years in the game and getting tenure at an amazing school district just outside of Philadelphia, I had become a well-respected, accomplished teacher. I honed my skills under some great mentoring, found my feet in test prep, and had gotten powerful and positive feedback from many students and parents. I'd grown and managed a large after-school theatre program. I'd made amazing friends and even started a band with a fellow teacher that became a community rallying point for the faculty (and a brilliant method for us to drink for free at shows on the weekend).

But I couldn't get the mistakes of my first year at another school out of my head.

Despite the struggles I'd had, I loved my first year of teaching. That gig was at a middle school just outside of Doylestown, PA. The kids were extraordinary and the work seemed so damn important because, well, it was. I'd tried hard as hell to be good at the job in that way many first year teachers do.

But at the end of my first year, I was fired.

To be fair, "fired" might be a strong word. I was let out to pasture in the early spring of my first year of teaching. I remember the look in my then principal's eyes as she told me I wouldn't be coming back. "You just don't seem to have the stuff for this," she told me, her usually softened southern accent now drawing sharply and slowly on the word "stuff." That first feather of doubt tickled and tortured me years later, as if she'd just said it yesterday.

Back to the phone call: though I wondered if I had it in me to do it, I surprised myself and blurted my answer. "Yes—let's do it. I'm in." And just like that, I would be leaving it all in Philly to take a chance in New York, in exactly the same way so many people have left one chapter to begin another.

When I informed my school, my boss at the time—a brilliant teacher named Denise James—took me aside for some parting words. She told me that she was sad I was leaving, which meant a lot to me.

But she did something else that had a profound impact on me. It changed the course of my career.

She said, "You are an incredibly talented teacher. I've been watching you for years and I see it. You work hard, you believe in your students, and you listen to them. Your future students and fellow teachers will be luckier than they know."

Then she mentioned a few things that she had seen me do over the four years that I had been there. She gave me specifics—she really watched me. She wasn't just trying to boost my ego or tell me nice things. She had clearly thought about me, paid attention to me, and had looked for what was good and strong about me.

And because of all of that, I believed her.

Suddenly, like with the wave of a wand, all the weight of my failure in my first year just slid away. Ms. James helped me see myself and, in doing so, helped me unlock the abilities that I didn't even acknowledge to myself. There's no way she could have helped me if she didn't spend time really knowing me. It filled me up, made me feel strong, and launched me with power and momentum into my next job. Her words still feed me today, almost two decades later.

Leader Growth Hormone

It is a very rare teacher, principal, superintendent or person who has overcome self-doubt. We all struggle with believing in ourselves, no matter how successful we become. In the secret fortresses of our minds, we tell ourselves stories about our limitations. The history of greatness is riddled with stories of heroes who can't get self-doubt out of their heads, even after success. John Steinbeck, before he won the Nobel Prize for Literature, wrote in his journal, "I am not a writer. I've been fooling myself and other people." Abraham Lincoln famously fought his own melancholy that he was not up to the job of being President. Tina Fey has described her struggle this way: "The beauty of the impostor syndrome is you vacillate between extreme egomania, and a complete feeling of: 'I'm a fraud!.'" Even the great Maya Angelou, whenever she published a new book of poetry, worried that she'd "run a game on everybody, and they're going to find [her] out."

As a leader, you have an extraordinary opportunity to hold up a golden mirror and reflect what is good and powerful about each of your teachers. In the intermittent cloudiness of their self-doubt, you can help them see their own greatness. This is among the most formidable tools in education, wielded by great teachers and leaders alike. It is the reason why renowned coaches can leave one winning team and lead another team to championships. Why an inspirational CEO can lead success from one company to another. Why a wise parent can dole out wisdom to more than one of her kids.

As educational leaders, our focus sets the tone and creates the culture in our schools. People are hungry to be seen and valued. Their flaws and mistakes should not be our top priority. Our job is to look for their gleaming ribbons of brilliance and amplify them. When a leader reaches the level of trust where she can look straight into the eyes of someone she leads and say, "I see great strength in you," it's like a shower of magic feathers suffocating their self-doubt.

These magic feathers won't give them magic wings but they will help them believe in their own talents and their potential to rise to the next level. As a leader, you must attend to their greatness. When you do, you give them a magic feather.

OTHERFUL PRINCIPLE

Your authentic belief in your people's capabilities
changes how they see themselves.

QUICK SKIM

Our bosses, coaches, teachers, and parents get special access to how we think about ourselves. They become a voice in our heads, a part of the conversation that each of us has with ourselves. It's happened to you. You can hear the voices of old teachers, can't you? Because each of us has a short list of mentors that impact how we think of who and what we are. These teachers stay with us long after we leave them. And, as a leader, you have the power to give that gift to others.

You never really know when a person is at an intersection in their lives when a word from a leader can create a tectonic shift in that person's sense of self. Recognize that you, as a leader, have an echoing, repeating voice in so many other people's heads. The best leaders can hold up a golden mirror to their people, and can say: "I see strength in you. So much potential. I believe in you."

And, when the leader says this, if she's spent the time to know them and gained their trust, they will believe it.

Believe that your people are great, or not great. You will be right, either way.

TRY THIS

- Recognize that, as the leader, your words to your people have special power. You can heal, hurt, grow, or stunt your teachers, colleagues, and students. It doesn't matter what your intentions are. It only matters how they take it.

- Spending time with your people doesn't just earn their trust. It unlocks their ability to believe you when you tell them great things about themselves. Without putting that time in, you invite them to question whether you mean that wonderful thing you just told them.

- Bet on the greatness of your people. It's amazing what people will do for a leader who believes in them. Transformational leadership is about alchemy, not mathematics. Put all your money on your people or get out of here already.

DISCLAIMER

You might be convinced that some of your people are, actually, not very good. That they are hitting their heads against the low ceiling of their abilities. And you might be right.

To be in charge, you must demand that your people maintain professional skills and proper techniques. In leadership, we must have criticism and painful conflicts. We do have to call people out sometimes. It happens.

But here's a short disclaimer to our disclaimer: educational leadership suffers from an over-emphasis on what we often refer to as "rigor." It's like we're all caught up in some game to prove to the teachers, the other admin, and the parents that we are tough, detailed, and not afraid to take somebody out. It's a reasonable temptation. Leadership myths persist in the world of administration and are almost always about leaders having a firm hand, a no-bullsh*t attitude, and a mistake free ledger. We all know at least one superintendent who is widely respected for being a ball-busting, never-an-error, "call a spade a spade" boss. It might be you. And maybe that's what you really crave. That's fine.

These leadership myths can drive us. But they can also stunt our greatest power.

Our point: the real, deep leadership magic isn't in "No, you can't."

It's in, "Yes, you can."

And we'll bet this whole book that somewhere in your past, someone helped you believe that about yourself. And that's at least part, if not largely, why you're a leader today.

YOU'RE THE BALM

Reason doesn't start with a clean slate on which our brains record their pure observation. Reason proceeds from choices to notice some things but not others, to include some things and exclude others, and to view the world in a particular way when other visions are possible.

—Debra Stone, *Policy Paradox*

Because of our embodied histories, much of the time our own responses to children are automatic. We open our mouths and our parents or our previous teachers come out. Changing our talk requires gaining a sense of what we are doing, our options, their consequences, and why we make the choices we make.

—Peter Johnston, *Opening Minds*

So, first of all, let me assert my firm belief that the only thing we have to fear is fear itself.

—Franklin Delano Roosevelt,
First Inaugural Address

No longer do balloons adorn a classroom door for a birthday or holiday party.

Some students have latex allergies. Our school district's Health and Wellness Committee recently released new guidelines, listing when and what food may be shared in classrooms. This has become common in schools. These allergies are dangerous, not only for children. A food allergy claimed the life of a family friend who was in his thirties. He accidentally ate the wrong thing at a party.

The sad irony of these allergies is that the body's misinterpretation of a harmless substance becomes harmful. There is no reason for a peanut to be lethal. It's the body's reaction to the thing rather than the thing itself that causes trouble.

The same is true in schools. Our reactions can be more harmful than the actions that precipitated them. Overreacting to a perceived threat can undermine everything you are doing. Your team cannot be resilient if they fear their leaders will overreact. In order to avoid harm, we would do well to examine why and how we react to things we identify as "a problem."

Why ask Why?

Often, we react to "problems" because:
1. ...we don't like what we see.
2. ...we are afraid other stakeholders won't like what they see in our reaction.

Our reactions can magnify or multiply the problems when:
1. **...we don't question whether what we don't like is truly problematic or, instead, just not our preferred style.** Others' actions sometimes lead to real problems. More often than we admit, though, others' actions are less problematic than they are at odds with our own sensibilities. There are lots of ways to do things. Being patient and taking the time to understand others' styles will save you a lot of unnecessary headbutting.

2. **...we react to quell our fear about judgment from other stakeholders if we don't act.** We'll know that parents or other admin are looking for a quick fix or a

scapegoat. Ironically, CYA type reactions, which we hope will protect us from ridicule, are often the ones that cost us the most. Capital built over years by listening and supporting teachers can be lost by reacting to CYA and making teachers feel left out in the cold.

It takes a brave leader to patiently react when a teacher has done something that would be viewed unfavorably by parents or other administrators. Sometimes, someone will report something to you with the expectation that you react strongly. Be careful. Most reactions here can undermine your culture of trust and growth. Unless you can demonstrate that you have your teachers' backs, they likely won't feel safe to take risks and try new things. You have the power to be the net under their tight rope. Don't give up that power to CYA.

It's Not A Disaster; It's "Sporty"

Anything that goes sideways can invite you and your school to have a terrible allergic reaction. This is your opportunity as a leader to use your immense power of renaming a situation. When we ran our theatre program together, we referred to urgent problems as "sporty." We saw something going not according to plan not as a threat but, rather, as a chance to try a new solution or rally the troops. Just by reidentifying a situation, we transformed how we saw and reacted to things.

Think about how you grade an incoming problem on a 1-10 scale with the higher number meaning a bigger, more dangerous problem. A problem that we call a 10, or even a 7 or 8, usually requires a 'survival mode' reaction—we must act quickly to protect the school (and/or ourselves) and destroy the threat. People will show up in your office or email box screaming "the sky is falling!" believing that the concern is a 10. Responding to the concern as if it were a 10 will cheat you of options—10s almost always lead directly to blame and censure.

There are almost no 10s.

If, on the other hand, we choose to identify a concern as a 4, we avoid the intensity and pressure of making whatever is happening go away right now. We can slow down, ask questions, confer, and reflect before we make a determination about the best way to move forward. The dialogue and reflection related to a concern that is a 4 can strengthen a team and increase the likelihood that the pre-cipitating concern is avoided in future. It's not about being nice or pretending things aren't as bad as they actually are. It's about being productively opportunistic with problems.

We constantly tell our students that mistakes are opportunities to learn. We should heed our own advice.

OTHERFUL PRINCIPLE

Our reactions to concerns can be productive or destructive.

QUICK SKIM

Leaders can decide what is a concern and how concerning it is. Our ability to deescalate is almost always more important than our ability to escalate. By treating problems as opportunities to learn, leaders can build strong relationships and resilient teams rather than tear a team apart and destroy trust.

TRY THIS

- Reflect on what you see as OK and not OK. How much of what you think is not OK is actually bad for students? Really bad? How much of what you see as not OK could be OK if you made room for it?

- When people come to you with something that they decided is not OK, don't be rushed to judgment and action. People might consider your lack of action as weakness, but your decision to reserve judgment is an action, one that requires strength and perseverance, particularly when people are spurring you.

- Just because someone thinks something is a 10 doesn't mean it's a 10. When people come to you listen, attend, and ask questions, but don't rush to reaction. A 10 leaves little room for dialogue and reflection.

DISCLAIMER

Sometimes you have to react swiftly, decisively, and with little mercy. Being the boss isn't always sunshine and roses; sometimes you need to be judge, jury, and executioner. There will be times when you have to go to Defcon 1, call the lawyers, and prepare for war. Don't ever forget that.

Just be careful with those nuclear codes. And be even more careful with your thinking. All reactions intended to judge, CYA, and/or punish usually deliver all sorts of collateral damage and concerns. Your reactions might induce a deadly inflammation for that culture of trust you've been working so hard to cultivate.

22 QUICK FIXES
TO CREATE THE
SCHOOL YOU WANT

ADMINISTRATOR LIFE EXPECTANCY

It's not a fresh start for your school when you get hired.

We should consider using a term to distinguish between administrator years and teacher years, just as we do between dog years and people years. Why? Administrators usually do not live as long in a school as teachers do.

Leaders often feel a sense of urgency to everything they want to accomplish. Unnecessary urgency is one of the most dangerous drivers in leadership. Eager to see a change and feeling like a change is taking too long, administrators may resort to artificial accountability tactics to mandate change—which, as we have noted earlier, tends instead to stifle change efforts by destroying trust.

Teachers and staff, grinding it out every day, are working on a different, slower timeline. The teachers and staff have been there for years (even veterans of only 1-2 years have experienced a lot of life at school before you showed up) and have lived through many administrators, each with his own idea about how things should work and his own improvement plan. 3-5 years after they arrive, these administrators often leave, replaced by another urgent fixer of the school. Even if you are not rushing to change people, it's likely that these teachers have had experiences with other administrators who have swooped in and tried to change them. So, you have to give teachers time to get to know you—to see that you mean what you say when you rely on natural accountability instead of artificial accountability.

Remember, you can't change anyone. You can only help them change themselves.

Just keep asking questions about the things you care about. Your teachers will be eager to understand what you care about—even when they feign not caring. That's what being the boss buys you. Pick the most important thing(s) and keep talking about them when you are with teachers. And wait and see.

Teachers move in teacher years, not administrator years. But if you're patient, you'll be surprised at how many teachers will work to figure out how to do what is important to you.

If you want to leave things better than you found them, then whatever you work to achieve has to belong to the teachers. Otherwise, as soon as you leave, it will be as if you were never there at all.

CALENDARS, YOURS AND THEIRS

What's on your teachers' calendars is more important than what's on yours.

Teachers live by daily class schedules. They often know, down to the minute, when they will pee. They attend to a relentlessly churning calendar that dominates their experience in school.

Think of it this way: if you are late to wherever you are going, you might have to apologize and explain what held you up. If your teacher is late for class, all kinds of things can happen.

Knowing and respecting your teachers' calendars screams loud and clear that they matter and you care about them.

How can you make sure you're getting calendars right?

1. **Underschedule yourself.** It's not enough to "have your door open." Schedule time in your calendar to just be present. You might be in your office or you might be walking around–able to respond to teachers' texts if they need you to come by. When your calendar is too full to allow teachers to drop in, then they can't drop in.

2. **Pay attention to your teachers' daily and yearly schedules.** Do they teach three in a row, in different rooms? Is it the end of the quarter? Are they preparing for midterms? Progress reports? Conferences? Do they have upcoming games, matches, science fairs, concerts, art exhibitions, plays, newspaper deadlines? Your folks are BUSY all the time.

The most impactful time you'll ever share with your teachers will not be when you are looking for them. It'll be when they are looking for you–and you actually had the time to be there for them.

COMPARING

Some people come to work early. Some work late. Some respond to emails quickly. Some are beautifully organized. Some work second jobs. Some are taking classes. Some have kids or parents that they take care of. Some always say "hello." Some workout.

Do as many good things as you can. Be proud of these things. But don't start noticing when people don't do the good things you do.

Who would want to work with someone who does that?

COMPLIMENTS FROM THE BOSS

There is a world of difference between a polite word and a real compliment. The former is a formality, the latter a performance-enhancing drug.

"DATA"

As we attempt to quantify every part of schooling and learning with measurable indicators, be wary. Things that cannot be described by numbers should not be described by numbers. A lot of the most important, actionable "data" in a classroom cannot be tortured into an integer, benchmark, zone, indicator, or anything else that looks good in a report.

Across fields, from the military to medicine to meteorology, the best leaders know that numbers only capture a slice of what is actually happening. Making "data" the supreme indicator of what's happening at your school makes everything else less meaningful and actionable.

That's why the professional commentary from a teacher/hall aide/specialist/bus driver/custodian is the most important data you should care about. Like the lookouts in the mountains of Aeschylus' Oresteia or Lassie scratching at the well, those who are working with and around students have the best data–their observations, thoughts, and intuitions.

There are few people more dangerous (or useless) in a school than a leader whose perfectly organized spreadsheets of "educational data" have made them comfortably numb.

HELP SOMEONE, HOW TO

No one really wants to be helped when they're not asking for it.

No matter how well intentioned you are or how badly a person's game begs for help, people want to be in control of the help they get. Think about that for a second. You hate unrequested help, too. The Founders of the United States referred to unrequested help from King George III as "tyranny."

But that doesn't mean you can't help people when you're the boss. It simply means that you need the consent of the governed.

Try this out at the beginning of the year:

Ask your people how they'd like to get suggestions from you. They can either respond:

1. I don't want your help, thank you very much.

2. Here's how you can tell me what and/or how to improve things...

Then, take their lead.

For the people who don't want your help, root for them, honestly, and be ready in case they change their minds about accepting that help you're trying to offer.

For the people who tell you how they'd like feedback, follow their parameters to the letter when you offer them help.

Treat your people like prize stallions and, by golly, many of them will start to act like it. Treat them like pack mules and don't be surprised when you get kicked in the gut, or worse.

HOOLIGANS

Sometimes people cause trouble in school. They show no respect for what you're trying to do and make you, the boss, feel like a fool. They push back at boundaries and sometimes the rules. They'll laugh behind your back and, sometimes, in front of you (during a meeting). Taking shots at you and the system, these troublemakers come in many forms:

> passive aggressive teachers,
> competitive administrators,
> recalcitrant staff members,
> belligerent parents,
> rebellious students, etc.

They'll cause you headaches and sap your energy from other work. They'll rile you up, get you steaming mad, and turn you into the worst version of yourself.

Remember this: it's not really about you. Even when it is about you.

In their own way, these stakeholders (because that's what they are) are pushing back for stuff they think is worth fighting for. To them, you're just the schlub in the way with the clipboard in your hands. And, even when you respond fairly, you won't always appease them. Sometimes you'll appease none of them.

But you can LEARN from all of them.

Have the guts to see that someone who is challenging you or the system is driven by the same thing you are: a desire for stuff to be better. Calling them "criminals" or "obstacles" doesn't help you. Instead, call them "hooligans" and let them teach you about yourself. You don't know what it feels like to get the screw from something you are leading. You'll have to take a few hooligans down, it's true. But mostly you should be glad that they illuminate that blindspot you have no idea you have. You should probably thank them.

Hooligans might also remind you to not take yourself so seriously. Sometimes it takes a wise-cracking jester to show the king that a crown is just another silly hat and that life is too precious to try and be right all the time.

HUMAN LIGHTNING RODS

Although Billy Joel, who often ends his concerts encouraging his audience not to take any sh*t from anybody, might disagree, the ability to take other people's sh*t without giving it back is among a leader's greatest capacities.

Most of the sh*t that ends up on the leader's desk is not of the leader's making. What is a leader to do? Fling it back? Things will get messy. The best leaders channel the sh*t that constantly gets thrown at them to where it belongs: into the ground where it can't hurt anyone.

Can't say "sh*t" in your staff meetings? Neither can we. So put it this way:

Lightning rods don't accept the damage of the strike—and they keep the building from catching on fire. Get it?

HUMOR, HAVING A SENSE OF

...and now for an Otherful limerick.

Do you remember that leader at school?
Who forgot an unforgettable rule:
       "If you ain't bringing money
        You better bring funny"
Because nobody likes to work for someone who doesn't have a
sense of humor.

INITIATIVES

Initiatives usually go something like this:

1. **The administration** sees something that they think is a problem, or they attend a conference where they see something cool. They think, "This is something we can fix/do." They get busy, thinking about how they will direct the initiative. They identify teachers who will be early adopters and design a professional development plan, chocked full of meetings and PD sessions. They hire a consultant.

2. **Teachers** hear about this 'new' thing at a faculty or department meeting.
   - **New teachers** take notes and read handouts about the initiative.
   - **Veteran teachers** don't–unless it is to prepare a defense. They have been here before. And this 'new' initiative sounds very similar to that initiative from six years and two administrators ago.
   - **Smart veteran teachers** feign interest and ask a few questions. Experience has taught them that there will be little/no follow up from the administration about this initiative. They can dive under this wave and wait for the next one.
   - **Honest veteran teachers** openly share their disdain, which the administrator interprets as laziness, closed mindedness, and/or an inability to deal with change.

3. After rollout, the initiative dies a slow death over 1-5 years before being replaced by a new initiative. And repeat.

And so, the initiative becomes part of the artificial accountability cycle, which undoes professionalism overtime or drives it underground into splinter cells or shadow departments.

How can you avoid this laundry cycle?

Take the time to know your teachers and authentically involve them in identifying problems and selecting initiatives, particularly if those initiatives are designed in a way that allows teachers to find their own way in.

And then ask your teachers how the efforts are going, how they know that, and how you can help. If you do this right, almost all initiatives will be driven by the teachers and you'll be doing what great coaches have been doing for millennia: watching proudly from the sideline, ready with water, towels, encouragement, or anything else they need.

KEEPING SCORE

You know how you can't stand that person on your staff?

It's the one who always looks for what's wrong and enlists others to criticize your ideas. Or that one who always fumbles what you tell him, no matter how clear you are. Or that other one who totally screwed you over in an interview/initiative roll out/meeting, etc.

Yeah, that one. It's OK to admit it. No one can hear you but us.

Well, you're keeping score. And that ain't good for you or anybody else. The "good ones" are scared they're next. The "bad ones" are playing musical chairs, hoping not to be stuck without a seat.

You can't always choose the army you go to battle with—but you have to be able to work with all of your people. If you've got it out for someone who works for you, you better fix that up by taking action.

The playbook for clearing the scoreboard is ancient. Pick any one of the following or mix and match, chief.

1. Apologize for being so dang critical
2. Forgive the criminal for the crimes
3. Admit an error you've made; share how dumb you felt
4. Laugh it off; diminish how big of a deal it is
5. Stop talking and thinking about it—MOVE ON

People will never stop disappointing you. So what? Did you sign up for leadership so you could judge everyone? Wait and see what they look like the next time YOU screw up.

When is that going to be, by the way?

Tomorrow?

Today?

L●VE

Nothing can replace the inimitable power of tenderness, compassion, forgiveness, and authentic concern for others when it comes from the boss.

There is no short cut, no hack here. If you consistently show love for your people, you will slowly and surely make your school a place of great dynamism and power. NOTE: Love is not being a "buddy" or a "cruise director," although people often respond well to someone who is nice.

Instead, love from the boss is a string of actions that make people feel like they are important. It's a series of decisions over time that gives everyone who works for you an anecdote or two of when you came through for them. It's the community-shared story of how wonderful it is to work with and for someone like you.

Love is
- writing a handwritten note with details
- sharing your fears and mistakes
- showing up without judgment
- taking second billing on a win
- finding the right moments to say
    "you should go home; I got this"
    "do you need a hug/beer/wingman/sounding board / break?"
    "what can I do for YOU?"
- remembering that a spouse is sick
- taking a punch from a parent on behalf of a teacher
- skipping an observation because someone's having a bad day

You want to get the best out of your people, right?

Leading with love means knowing that it's going to take the best of you to get it.

MEETINGS

Teachers meet all the time. They meet before school, after school, during school, with students and parents and other teachers. Many of them even talk together on weekends. So when administrators talk about having 'Meetings,' they are often only referring to the meetings they lead–often, the ones after school, the ones everyone is mandated to attend.

This is no bueno because:

- It devalues the many meetings teachers are already having.
- It makes just about everyone hate 'Meetings.'

Any meeting that your people are forced to attend threatens to diminish their trust that you know what you are doing. The real proof of the value of the meeting is whatever is happening in the heads of the attendees, not in yours.

So here's the deal: stop mandating "Meetings" unless the meetings can pass the following litmus test. THERE WILL BE NO MEETINGS UNLESS THEY ARE…

1. The Big Family meetings, like at the beginning and end of the year, and when something serious/magic/tragic happens. These meetings are special in how they bring everyone together–even sacred, at times– and will become unspecial every time you make everyone attend any other meeting.

2. A meeting where each and every person present is necessary (and their absence would endanger the value of the meeting to people other than you). Smart leaders do not call the whole school or department very often. The smarter move

is to have an explicit reason for why each person is called—and then only call those folks and let them do most of the talking. If they aren't talking, you shouldn't have called them. People should want to come to your meetings; if they don't, you're doing this wrong. And woe to you, worthy leader, if you mandate that people show "proof of work" done at a meeting by those who didn't want to go or didn't understand why the meeting even happened.

Have as many meetings as you want so long as they pass that test. Want to test our test? Make attendance voluntary and see who shows up.

If you are mandated to mandate meetings, mandate that your people meet about what they want and make yourself available if they want you. Don't make them produce something for you to prove that they did something. (Don't you hate when your bosses require that of you?) You will know you are gaining influence if you are able to walk in on a teacher-run meeting (or get invited to one) and the teachers keep talking about what they are actually talking about rather than stopping because you have come in.

People think and reflect best when they think and reflect together. Time reflecting with other educators is THE ABSOLUTE most valuable professional development. Your people have already determined whether or not you understand this truth by the way you call and conduct meetings.

The good news? You can change how you run the meetings—and start earning their trust— at any time, boss.

OBSERVATIONS

Though the biggest reason why we observe our teachers/colleagues is because we are required to do so, there are only two PRACTICAL purposes for a classroom observation:

1. To figure out how to help someone
2. To fire someone

If you don't know how to do #1 and you aren't interested in #2, make the observation and observation report as simple and painless as possible for both of you. Do not invent some way to "help" a person in order to prove that the time is not wasted.

Doing that, my friend, is the best way to waste time.

And don't you have a ton of other things to do?

PARENTS

Good relationships with parents are essential. Parents are the best allies and do great things for the school. Except when they don't.

When dealing with an obstreperous parent, remember:

1. **Parents are driven by an image they have** of what they want their children to be. This image may or may not be consistent with the children's or teachers' image. When the parents perceive that events are leading their children toward their image, they are happy and supportive. When the parents perceive that events are leading their children away from that image, they are afraid and potentially dangerous.

2. Parents will advocate/lobby for their children—**sometimes, at the expense of other people's children and/or teachers.** If you are not careful about your interactions with parents in these situations, you can destroy the trust you have cultivated with your teachers and/or other parents.

3. When parents contact you, **don't expect them to have all the information, be rational, or play by rules.** If they do any of those things, that's great. In the meantime, always work to deescalate and, when possible, create harmony. Even the most radicalized parents are driven to protect and support their children.

4. **Burning a teacher or colleague to appease a parent** is one of the most powerful ways to get people who work with you to dislike you. You can't always turn everyone into a winner, but you can often minimize the number of losers.

5. **Parent interactions can embed themselves in stories about you** in your community. You probably can't stop the negative stories they might tell about you. The smart move is to innoculate yourself by having as many good interactions with parents as you can.

It may help to remember that parents who make you crazy had parents, too—parents who may have taught them to behave this way. And then think of your own parents. It's a hard job—the hardest. And then maybe forgive them all.

PROGRESS, MAKING

Talking with Jerry Seinfeld on an episode of Comedians in Cars Getting Coffee, former President Obama compared the US Presidency to football, noting that most of one's time is spent fighting over inches, but that once in a while a president can find an opening and get something done.

So, for the rest of us leaders who don't have the nuclear codes, realizing that our work is often about inches rather than yards can save us a lot of angst.

Be careful about where you set your goalposts. One interaction, or even ten of them, will likely not change a person at school. Expectations like this are a recipe for wasted resources–and perhaps heartache.

The thing is, if the leader can stay patiently focused and directed long enough, the inches will add up to yards.

SCHOOL BOARDS

The time-honored school board may be one of the remaining vestiges from America's past dreams of civic engagement, but don't be fooled: the earth can be moved there. Board Meetings are usually structured around four things: performance (test scores), budgets, personnel, and controversy.

Those in the superintendency have to be political masterminds to ensure that those aspiring politicians on the board (and in the community) don't take the steering wheel from them. Make no mistake, negotiating with the school board is no different than the sausage making on the floor of the US Congress. If you are at the top of the chain, you know it already. It's a blood sport and it's your job on the line, over and over.

The most important work you do with the school board is being Master Translator (something we call "Contexting"). You need to constantly build context for people who don't have it. The key is to make sure that no one on the board ever feels wrong or humiliated. It's not that they don't get what's happening in school. They just don't quite see it in the right light, yet. That's where you come in.

Build and maintain relationships, listen like a lawyer, lose like an Olympian, win like a servant, and don't be afraid to laugh at yourself from time to time.

If you are a principal or department chair, well, you're there to be eye candy. Put on something nice and for heaven's sake, smile. Smile a lot and at everyone. Do your presentation on test scores, curriculum, or what have you. Remember, you're the face of that all-star production that everyone in town is always talking about: the major motion picture of your school. If you make people feel good about that movie, they'll feel a little less bad about how you guys keep making them pay for tickets year after year.

And remember, nothing brings down the house better than

a floor show starring the very best we got: our students singing, dancing, sharing their science projects, or, heck, just standing there.

SINGING, IN YOUR HEAD

You decided to be the leader. Now, you have to take the high road. All the time. It doesn't matter if lots of the folks you're dealing with are taking the low road. You cannot.

But, here's what you can do.

When you're feeling frustrated and you just want to tell this guy where he can go, you can sing in your head. NOTE: DO NOT SING ALOUD.

Pick a song that lets you get your frustration out, see it, laugh at it, and get back to the important work of taking the high road.

A favorite song choice for us is that old South Park chestnut "F*ck your F*cking Face, Uncle F*cker." But, really, any song will do.

TITLES, IN A HIERARCHY

Your title only guarantees one thing: for better or for worse, the people below you will pay attention to what you say and do.

Oddly, your title can make it harder to help your people grow. There are a number of reasons for this and some of them include that your title:

- does not deliver the respect of those below you, and any effort to earn respect with your title will backfire
- amplifies your people's distaste with you when you disappoint them
- makes it more difficult to offer constructive criticism

Your title will often be your greatest liability except when you:
- offer honest praise to those below you
- go first when claiming responsibility for team errors
- use it to help someone

The best thing about having a title, aside from the pride of your parents, is when your people trust you enough to actually forget that you have it.

TODAY (NOT TOMORROW)

As a leader at school, you need to keep your eye on the horizon. Many future requirements clamor for your attention: next year's budget (and the year after that), who's going to be staffing what classes, supply orders, new state and federal mandates... not to mention that job at another school that you're secretly eyeing up.

But tomorrow is also a never-ending distraction that keeps you from the only moment that actually exists: this moment right now. When you spend time with your teachers, parents, and students, they need your eye contact and full attention.

In hallways, before and after faculty meetings, and at chance encounters at the grocery store, those beautiful and flawed teachers (on whom the whole bloody system turns) need you to listen to their concerns, advice, dreams, and reports. An authentic connection with you—even one time in a year—can feed them for many months. Give them whatever attention you can.

And those glorious students, who grow from toddlers to young adults right in front of us, need our deliberate attention more than they need anything else. They need it each and every time you're there. There is no currency that you can spend more valuable than your precious attention. Light up when you see them! Those kids need you today, not tomorrow.

It's easy to get lost in the weeds. You'll be tempted to see the calendar as a drill sergeant who commands you to attend an endless series of meetings. You'll want to be aware of the clock all the time. And you should. Just don't forget to live in the present. Look around! See where you are right this moment. Like the school system itself, you need to plan for tomorrow but live (and lead) fully in today.

TRUST

When the boss says,
"Do what I tell you. I'll be watching to make sure you do it,"
then people will do things when the boss is watching. When the
boss isn't watching, all bets are off.

When the boss says,
"Trust yourself. Just try to always do what you think is right. If
you mess up, we'll learn from it and do better next time,"
then people will trust themselves, do their best, and learn from
their mistakes.

Which boss gets better results? Your call.

WRONG, SEEING WHAT'S

There will be times when you see the beauty in everything and times when you see what is wrong with everything.

Beware seeing what is wrong with everything. It happens to every leader. These times are like full moons for a werewolf. You will have the potential to do a lot of damage.

Take precautions.

As soon as you notice you have the stink eye coming on:

1. Avoid settings where you have to make decisions.
2. If you have to meet with other people, try only to listen. Wait to make decisions until you are out of this state.
3. Identify some jobs that are terrible and don't pay well. Remind yourself how happy you are not to be doing those jobs.
4. List the benefits of your job.
5. Think about what is good about the people with whom you work.
6. Breathe.

ACKNOWLEDGMENTS

**THINK WHERE MAN'S GLORY MOST BEGINS AND ENDS,
AND SAY MY GLORY WAS I HAD SUCH FRIENDS.
—WILLIAM BUTLER YEATS**

We want to thank the many teachers and students who've believed in us, often when we didn't believe in ourselves. And we'd be sunk without naming the amazing people in our families who will undoubtedly recognize themselves and each other in this book. A special thanks to Karen Stewart for keen-eyed editing and Kellie McGann for placing each and every word.

There are so many people who have impacted us and our thinking, and we'd never be able to name them all. But we'll try to name a few. Thanks to our immediate and beautiful families: Bill, Marilyn, Will, Kelly, Sean, Colleen, Abigail, Quinn, and Molly O'Hara; Bridget, Stephen, Jack, and Dylan Kaplan; Molly Winter Stewart, John, Jane, Paul, Kate, and Sarah Kleba. And to our friends, colleagues at North Shore and Oyster Bay-East Norwich Schools, former teachers, and more family, including: Nancy Letts, Tony Scimone, Laura Seinfeld, Lisa Mulhall, Joe Pesqueira, Janna Ostroff, Sabrina Meehan, Sharon Lasher, Valerie Vacchio, Tami McElwee, Lara Gonzalez, Peter Rufa, Jack Burke, Tim McCarthy, Rebecca Menuzzo, Kevin Leach, Kevin Trentowski, Marisa Bel, Darlene Dolan, Mike Rispoli, Richard Bernato, Anthony Annunziato, Dennis O'Hara, Lydia Brady, Karen DiMaggio, Brian Donohue, Deirdre Faughey, Laura Keenan, Maria Kim, Shannon

Murphy, Nicole Schwartz, Chris Weber, Margaret Mastrogiacomo, Maria Randazzo, Lisa Tipere, Megan Galioto, Tracy Zambelli, Erin Dubon, Chris Bartell, Roseann Rehill Davidson, Kat Schechter, Peter Giarrizzo, Chris Zublionis, Olivia Buatsi, Kevin Kurrus, Albert Cousins, Jennifer Imperiale, Julie Ritter, Dalia Rodriguez, Amy DiMeola, Seth Gordon, Ed Melnick, Rob Chlebicki, Marc Ferris, Rachel Green, Brian Nelson, Kyrie Siegel, Michael Kerschner, Alex Goodman, Maram Mabrouk, Josh Knight, Michael Bishop, Elliot Touretz, Josh Timlin, Jason Domingo, David Soto, Lisa Polito, Sarah Hogan, Joanne Fawcett, Janine Gibstein, Anita Demitri, Christopher Letts, Ro Filone, John Jackson, Michael Dunn, Keith Slack, Jessica McKinney, Dave Keenan, Lauren Mistretta, Terryl Donovan, Melinda Bloom, Rick Bloom, Marianne Russo, Julia Brennan, Kevin Wallace, Troy Kreiner, Elliott French, Rebecca and Peter Warzer, Tim Fricke, Eli Staudt, Coleman Mellett, AnnMarie Sandy and her family, Jason Fuges, Josh Koll, Sarah Siplack, Scott Peterson, Rene and Bill Peoples, Chris Mancini, Brian Sauls, Danielle Dybiec, Chip Hill, Gary Slifkey, Pat and Lauren Burke, Nithya Rajendran, Brian Lucraze, Judy and Les Herman and family, Susan Rigler and family, The Eberts, The Stewarts, The Hillers, The Alberti, Chris Burcin, Rev. Donald McEachin, Rev. Dan Sormani, Sister Rosa Mystica, Ms. Vadosky, Bud Stock, Rev. Joseph Rymdeika, Judy Owens, Michelle Murphy, Jim Ferris, Ed Dobry, Raj Sheddy, John Worthington, Denise James, Donna Jackson, Kathy Kane, Jenny Perry, Dave Simpson, Chris Hamsher, Kathy Tyson, Justin Sitron, Eileen Fernandez-Parker, Jeff Roth, Ron Reed, Greg Rosenbaum, the whole SXSWedu team and family, Jessica Millstone, James Miles, Eric Nentrup, Andrew Smith Lewis, Noah Blumenthal, Dan Greenwald, Nick Kurian, Shamil Rodriguez, Caleb Gandara, Phil Egelston, John Tidwell, Nicole LaFontaine, Mary Ehrenworth, Shanna Schwartz, Tom, Ann, Thomas, Claudia, and Karem Kenny, Jim, Patrice, Stephen, Tara, and Shamus Davidson, Joyce Kenny, Molly McGonigle, Charlie and Debbie Hamilton, Ian Rasmussen, Ken Kuzma, Dawn Zacchino, Pat Kobel, Harriet Power, Earl Bader, Rev. Peter Donohue, Michael Hollinger, Kathleen Gosnell, John Lane, Jay Keenan, and, of course, Wayne Scattergood.

WE'RE STANDING ON THE SHOULDERS OF GIANTS

SOURCES AND REFERENCES

The Animals. (1965). Please don't let me be misunderstood. *Animal tracks.* New York: Columbia Records.

Anouilh, J. (2010). *Antigone.* New York: Samuel French.

Argyris, C. & Schon, D. (1974). *Theory in practice: increasing professional effectiveness.* San Francisco: Jossey-Bass.

Benjamin, B., Caldwell, G., Marcus, S. (1964). Please don't let me be misunderstood. *Broadway, Blues, Ballads by Nina Simone.* Amsterdam: Philips.

Berger, J. (1973). *Ways of seeing.* New York: The Viking Press.

Berry, J. W., Worthington, E. L., Parrott, L., O'Connor, L. E., & Wade, N. G. (2001). Dispositional forgivingness: development and construct validity of the transgression narrative test of forgivingness (TNTF). *Personality and Social Psychology Bulletin*, 27(10), 1277–1290.

Bloom, H. (2003). *John steinbeck.* Philadelphia : Chelsea House Publishers.

Bohm, D. (2004). *On dialogue.* New York: Routledge Classics.

Bolman, L.G. & Deal, T.E. (2013). *Reframing organizations*, 5th ed. San Francisco: Jossey-Bass.

Bondi, H & Samuel, J. (1997). The lense–thirring effect and mach's principle. *Physics Letters A.* 228 (3): 121. Cambridge, UK: Elsevier.

Bourdain, A. (2000). *Kitchen confidential: adventures in the culinary underbelly.* New York: Harper Collins.

Carnegie, D. (1998). *How to win friends and influence people: the only book you need to lead you to success.* New York: Gallery Books.

Cochran-Smith, M. & Lytle, S.L. (1993). *Inside outside: teacher research and knowledge.* New York: Teachers College Press.

Cochran-Smith, M. & Lytle, S.L. (2001). *Taking an inquiry stance on practice.* In A. Lieberman. & D. Miller (eds.). *Teachers caught in the action: professional development that matters.* New York: Teachers College Press.

Cochran-Smith, M. & Lytle, S.L. (2009). *Inquiry as stance: practitioner research for the next generation.* New York: Teachers College Press.

Cochran-Smith, M. & Lytle, S.L. (2006). Troubling images of teaching in no child left behind. *Harvard Educational Review*, 76(4), 668-726.

Colton, A.B. & Sparks-Langer, G.M. (1993). A conceptual framework to guide the development of teacher reflection and decision making. *Journal of Teacher Education*, 44(1), 45-54.

Covey, S.R. (2004). *The seven habits of highly effective people: powerful lessons in personal change.* New York: Free Press.

Dahlberg, K.R. & Philippot, R.A. (2008). The power of collaboration: a case for teachers helping to determine professional development agendas. *Planning and Changing*, 39 (1), 21-41.

Darling-Hammond, L. & Mclaughlin, M.W. (1999). Investing in teaching as a learning profession: policy problems and prospects. In L. Darling-Hammond & G. Sykes (eds.), *Teaching as the learning profession: handbook of policy and practice* (pp. 376-411). San Francisco: Jossey-Bass. de Saint-Exupéry, A. (1934). Night flight. New York: Harcourt Press.

Dewey, J. (1938). *Experience and education.* New York: Simon & Schuster.

Dewey, J. (1933). *How we think.* Boston: DC Heath & Company.

Dickens, C. (2009). *A christmas carol: and other christmas books.* New York: Everyman's Library.

Eisenhower, D. (1948). *Crusade in europe.* New York: Doubleday.

Emdin, C. (2016). *For white folks who teach in the hood-- and the rest of y'all too: reality pedagogy and urban education.* Boston, MA: Beacon Press.

Exline, J.J. & Baumeister, R. (2000). Expressing forgiveness and repentance: benefits and barriers. In M.E. McCullough, K.I. Pargament & C.E. Thoresen (Eds), *Forgiveness: theory, research and practice* (p. 133 - 155). New York: Guilford.

Fast, A. (2015). *It's the mission, not the mandates: defining the purpose of public education.* Lanham, MD: Rowman & Littlefield.

Freire, P. (2000). *Pedagogy of the oppressed.* New York: Bloomsbury

Gawande, A. (2007). *Better: a surgeon's notes on performance.* New York: Picador.

Hargreaves A. & Fullan, M. (2012). *Professional capital: transforming teaching in every school.* New York: Teachers College Press.

Heider, J. (1986). *The tao of leadership.* Atlanta, GA: Humanics Limited.

Hill, L. (1999). Everything is everything. *the miseducation of lauryn hill.* New York: Columbia.

Holy Bible. (1999). *King james version.* New York: American Bible Society.

Holy Bible. (1990). *New revised version.* New York: Harper Collins.

Irving, J. (1999). *The cider house rules.* New York: Modern Library.

Johnson, P. H. (2012). *Opening minds: using language to change lives.* Portland, ME: Stenhouse Publishers.

Kahane, A. (2007). *Solving tough problems: an open way to talking, listening, and creating new realities.* San Francisco: Berret-Koehler Publishers.

Kahane, A. (2017). *Collaborating with the enemy: how to work with people you don't agree with or like or trust.* Oakland, CA: Berret-Koehler Publishers.

Lahey, J. (2015). T*he gift of failure: how the best parents learn to let go so their children can succeed.* New York: HarperCollins.

Langley, N. (1939). *The wizard of oz.* Hollywood, Calif.: Metro Goldwyn Mayer, 1939.

Lee, H. (2002). *To kill a mockingbird.* New York: HarperCollins.

Lencioni, P. (2002). *The five dysfunctions of a team: a leadership fable.* San Francisco, Jossey-Bass.

Loesser, F. (1950). A bushel and a peck: *guys & dolls.* London: Decca.

McCormack, M. (2014). *What they don't teach you at harvard business school.* London: Profile Books Ltd.

Miller, A. (2003). *All my sons: a drama in three acts.* New York: Penguin Books.

Misner, Charles W., Kip S. Thorne, and John Archibald Wheeler. (1973). *Gravitation.* San Francisco: Freeman.

Morrison, T. (1998). *Beloved.* New York: Vintage Books

National Research Council. (2000). *How people learn: brain, mind, experience, and school.* Washington D.C.: National Academy Press.

Osterman, K.F. & Kottkamp, R.B. (2015). *Reflective practice for educators: professional development to improve student learning.* New York: Skyhorse Publishing.

Puzo M. & Coppola F. (1972). *The godfather.* Los Angeles: Paramount.

Pringle, G. (2010). Tina Fey—From spoofer to movie stardom. *Independent.*

Rage Against the Machine. (1992). Killing in the name. *rage against the machine.* Los Angeles: Epic.

Robbins, A. (1997). *Unlimited power : the new science of personal achievement.* New York: Free Press.

Robinson, K. (2001). *Learning to be creative.* Oxford, UK: Capstone Publishing.

Sahlberg, P. (2011). *Finnish lessons: what the world can learn from educational change in finland.* New York: Teachers College Press.

Schein, E.H. (2013). *Humble inquiry: the gentle art of asking instead of telling.* San Francisco: Berret-Koehler Publishers.

Schein, E.H. (2010). *Organizational culture and leadership, 4th ed.* San Francisco, Jossey-Bass.

Schon, D. (1987). *Educating the reflective practitioner.* San Francisco: Jossey-Bass.

Schon, D. (1983). *The reflective practitioner: how professionals think in action.* New York: Basic Books.

Senge, P. et. al. (2012). *Schools that learn.* New York: Crown Publishing.

Senge, P. (1990). *The fifth discipline: the art & practice of the learning organization.* New York: Double Day.

Shakespeare, W. (2002). *William shakespeare: the complete works.* New York: Penguin.

Shulman, L.S. (2004). *The wisdom of practice: essays on teaching, learning, and learning to teach.* San Francisco: Jossey-Bass.

Simon, C. (1971). You're so vain: *no secrets.* London: Trident Studios.

Sincero, J. (2013). *You are a badass: how to stop doubting your greatness and start living an awesome life.* Philadelphia: The Running Press.

Sparks-Langer, G.M. & Colton, A.B. (1991). Synthesis of research on teachers' reflective thinking. *Educational Leadership,* 48(6), 37-44.

Springsteen, B. (1985). I'm on fire: *born in the u.s.a.* New York: Columbia.

Stone, D. (2012). *Policy paradox: the art of political decision making,* 3rd ed. New York: W.W. Norton & Company.

Stone, D & Heen, S. (2014). *Thanks for the feedback: the science and art of receiving feedback well.* New York: Penguin Books.

Suzuki, S. (2006). *Zen mind, beginner's mind.* Boston, MA:

Shambhala.

Taleb, N. (2010). *The black swan.* New York: Random House.

Tarazi, B. (2012). *The accountability effect: the book your excuses don't want you to read.* CreateSpace Independent Publishing Platform.

Townsend, R. (1970). *Up the organization: how to stop the corporation from stifling people and strangling profits.* New York: Fawcett Crest Books.

Wallace, C. (1994). Juicy: *ready to die.* New York: Bad Boy Records.

Walker, A. (2004). *In search of our mothers' gardens: womanist prose.* New York: Mariner Books.

Walsh, B. & DaGradi, D. (1964). *Mary poppins.* Burbank, CA: Buena Vista.

Warrell, M. (2014). Afraid of being 'found out?' how to overcome impostor syndrome. *Forbes magazine.*

Weiner, M. (2010). The suitcase: *mad men.* Los Angeles: Warner Brothers.

Whyte, D. (2002). *The heart aroused: poetry and the preservation of the soul in corporate america.* Revised Edition. New York: Currency Doubleday.

Wilder, T. (2003). *Our town: a play in three acts.* New York: Perennial.

Witvliet, C.V.O., Ludwig, T. E., & Vander Laan, K. L. (2001). Granting forgiveness of harboring grudges: Implications for emotion, physiology, and health. *Psychological Science,* 12, 117-123.

Wojcicki, E. (2019). *How to raise successful people: simple lessons for radical results.* New York: Houghton Mifflin Harcourt.

Zeichner, K.M. & Liston, D.P. (1996). *Reflective teaching: an introduction.* Mahwah, New Jersey: Lawrence Erlbaum Associates.

Zhao, Y. (2012). *World class learners: educating creative and entrepreneurial students.* Thousand Oaks, California: Corwin.

ABOUT THE AUTHORS

Mike Kleba has been a public high school English teacher and theatre director for more than 20 years. An artist and entrepreneur, he is co-organizer of the NYEdTech Meetup, sits on the SXSWedu Advisory Board, and has been invited to speak about teacher-led innovation around the country and overseas. Interested in courage and vulnerability, he's run the NYC Marathon, gone hang-gliding in Brazil, bungee jumped in New Zealand, and climbed Mt. Kilimanjaro. Kleba lives with his wife and dog in Brooklyn, NY, and believes that all great leaders act like great teachers.

Ryan O'Hara, Ed.D., taught high school and middle school English for 10 years before moving into educational leadership. Before teaching, he apprenticed at Williamstown Theater Festival and performed in a national tour of *Tartuffe* and an American Globe production of *Our Town* in NYC. Dr. O'Hara currently works as a district administrator for a K12 public school district, where he busks in the halls with his fiddle and tin whistle on holidays, recites Seamus Heaney and William Shakespeare to all who need inspiration, and strives to spot greatness in others. He lives with his wife, who is a school principal, and three daughters on Long Island.

Ryan and Mike are great friends. This is their first book.